THE
Heart
Reconnection

GUIDEBOOK

A GUIDED JOURNEY OF PERSONAL
DISCOVERY AND SELF-AWARENESS

MARY FAULKNER AND **LEE MCCORMICK**

WITH JOAN BORYSENKO, PhD,
WILL TAEGEL, PhD AND GARY SEIDLER

PRACTITIONER'S GUIDE BY HOLLY COOK, LPC

Health Communications, Inc.
Deerfield Beach, Florida

www.hcibooks.com

**Library of Congress Cataloging-in-Publication Data
is available through the Library of Congress**

© 2018 Mary Faulkner and Lee McCormick

ISBN-13: 978-07573-2125-2 (Paperback)
ISBN-10: 07573-2125-9 (Paperback)
ISBN-13: 978-07573-2126-9 (ePub)
ISBN-10: 07573-2126-7 (ePub)

HCI, its logos, and marks are trademarks of Health Communications, Inc.

Publisher: Health Communications, Inc.
            3201 S.W. 15th Street
            Deerfield Beach, FL 33442–8190

Cover design by Ted and Peggy Raess, www.raessdesign.com
Interior design and formatting by Lawna Patterson Oldfield

Contents

Prologue
Return to the Great Mystery

From our earliest beginnings, human beings have had a spiritual impulse; it's been referred to as the "God gene." We seek truth and meaning, qualities that are found in sacred territory. The earliest cultures imagined these qualities in the form of Great Mother and worshipped her as a loving and nurturing presence. Before we shifted from a mystical understanding of existence to a scientific one, we knew that the earth was a living being and that the Great Mystery was present in the forces of nature and in the heart and soul of the people. We lived in a world of connection and wholeness. We looked beyond the literal physical presentations of illness to the spiritual or mystical realms for solutions to our ailments.

Indigenous cultures have always understood disease to be the result of an imbalanced relationship. Balance is not a static condition. Rather it is an action that's always in motion, shifting, adjusting, and readjusting—balancing. Tribal life was organized around the principle of balancing and maintaining respectful kinship with the forces of nature.

In earlier times, we lived close to the land and experienced the interrelatedness of nature. We understood ourselves through relationship to our clan or tribe. In these early cultures, there was no concept of an individual separate from the whole; we drew our identity from the community. Our heart was wired for connection, relationships, the importance of place, and sacred presence. Although our conscious mind has forgotten this, our heart remembers.

Our flesh-and-blood heart exists within us as a physical form, and it exists in an unlimited way throughout the realms of the universe as an energetic field beyond physical restrictions. It is in relationship with everything else. From the stars to microbes to the ground we stand on, all creation exists in relationship—this is the sacred web of life.

Today, quantum field theory describes this principle as the unified field in which everything exists in a dynamic, expanding, vibrating universe of waves and particles. This living cosmos announces itself in a rhythmic pulse that is not unlike our own heartbeat. The fabric of the universe is a collection of cohesive fields vibrating, rising in waves of potential, manifesting in material patterns and forms and collapsing back into itself as it has done since the beginning of time. Don Lincoln, senior experimental physicist at the Fermi National Accelerator Laboratory, describes quantum fields as follows:

> Quantum fields are a mind–bending way of thinking.
> Everything, and that means everything is the consequence
> of many infinitely large fields vibrating. The entire universe
> is made of fields playing a vast subatomic symphony.
> Physicists are trying to understand the melody.[1]

---

1 *The Good Vibrations of the Quantum Field Theories, The Nature of Reality, the physics of nothing, everything and all things in between.* pbs.org, August 5, 2013.

Even as our culture became blind to the interrelatedness of all things and the sacredness of the heart, the Great Mystery played on. The shift toward a scientific mechanistic worldview occurred over the course of hundreds of years, reaching a peak in the seventeenth and eighteenth centuries. Western culture's interpretation of the universe shifted from heart centered to mind centered, and our more logical, less feeling, less intuitive side became dominant.

The mechanistic worldview saw the earth as an object over which humans have dominance. An emphasis was placed on acquiring knowledge and weighing, measuring, and categorizing all aspects of material existence. Religion replaced faith, and what we know in our hearts was forced to yield to dogma. Judgment and rules took the place of common sense and intuition. We perceived God as separate from us and from nature.

Our Western culture was organized on this worldview, and although the shift to quantum reality began in the early twentieth century, the basis of the mechanistic view still informs the systems and structures of society. It sees humans as superior to the natural world, not recognizing that we are nature. It sees humans and nature in a battle for survival.

While science has made great strides in terms of physical health and conveniences, the emphasis continues to be on beating diseases and ignoring the conditions in which these diseases flourish. The problem lies in the inability to see the connectedness of all things. We gather data and we know things, but we don't complete the circuit by grounding the knowledge in life—in our hearts. As a result, our culture is disconnected from the heart and the values of the heart. It is our task to come back to the heart and heal the circumstances of our personal lives that created heartbreak and disconnection. In doing so, we honor our spiritual nature, shift our community toward true health and healing, create space for others to join with us, and, most important, reestablish a connection with our heart.

While we cannot literally disconnect from our heart (it is always part of us) nor can we really break it, we can lose our awareness of its power to love, its sacredness, its willingness to forgive, and its ability to heal. We often turn our back on our awareness out of self-preservation or simply to fit into our culture or our family, but in that disconnection, we also lose sight of the buried patterns and the toxic emotions we carry within. By reconnecting with our heart and regaining this awareness, we are able to process, clear, and release these wounds from our body. By recovering faith in our true self through healing practices and reclaiming balance in our lives, we can come to know our true innate power and potential as self-healers. This is a journey into the Great Mystery of your heart and soul.

Reawakening the Wisdom of the Heart

Your heart knows the way.
Run in that direction.

~Rumi

The heart is the first organ in the body to function. It is beating even before the brain is formed. The heart instructs the mind in the ways of balance and right relations. The challenge lies in believing your heart and following its wisdom when you have to go against generations of conditioning to do that. An awakened heart wants you back in touch with yourself. It wants you to believe in you.

1

We disconnect from our heart for many reasons, but when boiled down to their essence, they are variations on one theme: "I'm not good enough as I am." You may not be aware that you feel that way, as this feeling can become second nature. You may not fully realize how it holds you back or creates that restlessness that eventually propels you into some kind of self-defeating behavior. "Not good enough" is a lie undermining everything you do or attempt to do. Your heart knows it's a lie, but in that disconnection, your mind can't get the message. Healing begins the moment you return to your heart and remember that not feeling good about yourself is the only thing that's not good enough.

Living in Harmony and Balance

A new relationship with yourself, with others, with all living creatures, and with the earth is in order. The old metaphor of the earth as dispirited and mechanical has given way to the reawakened memory of harmony, balance, relationship, and connection. This relationship is captured in the story we offer on pages 3–5, which was inspired by the title of a book by Dr. Will Taegel: *The Sacred Council of Your WILD HEART*.

Qualities of the heart can't always be proven scientifically, and they don't need to be proven to be real. Love has its own logic. Stories give us permission to talk about important things without the data to back them up; they are a fun, non-threatening way to convey extraordinary ideas. For us, "Wild Heart" represents our original, unconditioned, natural self—free of any voices that tell us we are not good enough.

A STORY FROM
BEYOND THE PALE

Wild Heart was sitting on a stump at the edge of time. She reached up and snapped off a twig from the nearby dogwood and began chewing on it. She motioned for us to come closer. We approached tentatively at first, but then more quickly. She drew us to her. This is what we discovered:

Communication with Wild Heart is intuitive. She knows what is in our heart and helps us find it. Wild Heart is an image of our unconditioned, authentic self, and she is in love with us. Don't bother trying to find the logic in that—Wild Heart lives beyond reason. She holds the deep wells of wisdom that have been with us since the beginning of time. She is our internal wilderness untouched by social conditioning. She is our instinctual and intuitive self. She is the feminine and the masculine in each of us and lives in the human heart of all genders.

She is our connection to the web of life, where we can retrieve our survival skills that show us the way home when we are lost, awaken us when we have grown dull to life, and free us when we have been kidnapped by the glitz and glory of too much culture. She is the fire in all acts of creativity. Clarissa Pinkola Estés talks about the absolute importance of this archetype to our psyche and we draw on her images. In her book *Women Who Run With the Wolves*, she reminds us that it is our Wild Woman who guides us along the ancient pathways of human existence. Wild Heart belongs to that tradition.

Wild Heart prefers the company of wolves to people. She thinks people act funny—not funny like *amusing,* but funny like *strange.* They work long hours, and then go home and watch TV. They have forgotten the feeling of sand or green grass between their toes. She says they are prisoners in their own mind. Her wolves are the symbol of all things wild and free. She said that when a wolf gets caught in a hunter's trap, it chews off its foot to get away—the wolf has the willingness to go to any lengths to be free. It is Wild Heart who awakens the part of us that will spring up and free ourselves from whatever trap we find ourselves, no matter the cost.

Wild Heart is the primal instinct that beats in the collective human heart, connecting us together as a tribe. She is our connection to archetypal Great Mother Earth from whom we take our human form. She reminds us of what we have forgotten, where we come from, and what we must do to thrive. She isn't talking about simply living through some disaster. She's talking about living authentically day by day, surviving the culture of consumerism that threatens to chew us up like the dogwood twig in her mouth. She takes it out of her mouth and waves it in front of our eyes to make her point!

It is Wild Heart who tells us to sharpen our instincts, to sniff the wind with the prowess of a wolf sensing the presence of a predator. It is she who whispers in our ear when we are sleeping, "If you are to make it in this world, wake up." Just as we remind children to buckle their seat belts, she reminds us to buckle up our connection with our heart where we will find the courage to live the life that is in us.

Wild Heart, with her instinctual love of the untamed, exists in the uncultured, unpaved places where the heart of the Great Mother is experienced. And she lives in the uncultured, unpaved places in our psyche where our truth and true creativity are found.

When we lose conscious connection with our Wild Heart, we feel lost. We can be easily tricked or manipulated. We'll settle. Or the opposite: we'll try to control, cajole, and take more than our fair share. We cave when we should stand strong and boast when we should keep still. We are off center, off our mark, unsure, confused, ashamed, stuck, without inspiration, flat, tired, and we don't follow through. Our voice is shaky and trails off at the end. We don't say what is on our mind. We hedge. Our eyes look downward.

Wild Heart knows beyond all doubt that we can recover from whatever situation or condition we have fallen prey to by connecting with the web of life where our survival skills are kept. She carries the consciousness of connection, courage, and creativity. She is our awakened response to the threat of extinction that we face individually when self-hate tightens its stranglehold on us and the threat of extinction we face as a species on the planet at this time in history. She is awakening each individual heart, synchronizing us together and focusing us on living a life that we find meaningful, one that makes sense to us. She reminds us that we have the ingenuity and drive to not merely cling to a rock and survive, as our cells once did, but to tap into that instinct and plant our roots back into the earth where we can thrive.

The Wildness of Our Heart

When we reconnect with the wildness of our heart, our uncondi-tioned selves, it takes us beyond misidentifications, beyond the self-limiting beliefs we have bought into and beyond the behaviors that do not reflect our truth. We are left stripped clean, scratching our head, and wondering what just happened. According to "Wild Heart" logic, stripping and wondering are great gifts! Being stripped of the world's idea of who you are and cleaned of what the world says you should do about it is the ultimate liberation and salvation.

In our society, we've been conditioned to think of the wilderness as an antisocial dark force that disrupts our plans. The only part of the foregoing sentence that's true is "disrupts our plans"! Wilderness doesn't care about plans, and in that liberating zone of neutrality, we can experience freedom.

> Re-examine all you have been told
> at school, at church, or in any book, dismiss
> what insults your own soul, and your very
> flesh shall be a great poem.
>
> ~Walt Whitman

Self-Inquiry Powers the
Journey Around the Wheel

As the poet says, it is wise to examine what you've been told and claim only that which affirms your truth. Self-inquiry awakens inner wisdom. "What would it be like if ...?" is a question that takes you deep into your heart and into the healing process. Here's a more specific question: "What would it be like if I was living the life I want to live?" And a thought-provoking one: "Am I living the life I want to live?"

Life as a human being is as amazing as it is complicated. We are beings of light, yet we have our body, mind, and emotions to contend with. We can be hurt, we can experience pain, we can heal, and we can be immensely joyful. We can do great things, and we can lose our way. At those times, we forget who we are, and we stop trusting in ourselves. We are disconnected and disoriented. Our confusing behaviors signal (subtly or glaringly) that we need help. We need a "road map" that can reconnect us to our heart and lead us back to our truth. The medicine wheel is such a map.

The medicine wheel will take you full circle, back to yourself and into new territory. You will walk the journey with others, but you will have your own experiences of that journey, your own perspectives, and your own unique awakening. On this journey, you will learn to listen to others, and others will learn to listen to you from the heart. This is where the common experience of being a human connects us through love, empathy, and compassion.

Healing takes on additional significance when it stops being a collection of interventions and protocols, and instead holds space and allows wisdom to speak. Holding space means opening your heart, trusting your intuition, claiming your power, letting go of judgment, and staying present during your process of self-inquiry. Holding your truth while you listen to someone else's truth is an art that develops as you become firmly reconnected to your own heart.

Here is a glimpse of what happens when you follow this wisdom path:

- You learn the power of questions.
- You learn to see yourself apart from your thoughts, judgments, fears, and story.
- You realize you are as much mystery as you are fact.
- You are not your body, mind, or emotions; rather, you are the one experiencing these aspects of being human.
- You set your intentions, assessing and adjusting them as you gain insight.
- You connect to your intuition and the natural world.
- You celebrate the diversity of your community of seekers.
- Your self-inquiry promotes personal growth, self-understanding, and self-love.
- You connect with your instinctive healing abilities through engagement with nature, creative expression, art, music, writing, meditation, relaxation, and conscious dreaming.
- You partake in a "good medicine" combination of healthy food, adequate rest, regular exercise, and respectful relations.
- You learn to sit with your questions, allowing deeper answers to come that bring insight into your true nature.

Reclaiming
Our Wholeness

This universe is not outside of you.
Look inside yourself; everything that you want,
you already are.

~Rumi

Why is it that all the good qualities of human nature are often attributed to God and the worst characteristics are usually attributed to human nature? For thousands of years, Western culture encouraged us to renounce the world and turn our gaze toward heaven. Somehow, earth and the physical body became the "enemy," and we were forced to make the impossible choice between our human nature and the divine. Thus, our mind-body became disconnected from our spirit. We were taught to think in terms of either/or, but this divisive thinking limits creative problem-solving. It also creates a feeling of separation of mind and spirit—a separation that does not exist in creation. Reconnecting with our heart helps us remember who we are and what we came here to do.

When we are connected to our heart, we acknowledge *both/and*. Things can be *both* one way *and* any number of other ways. Rather than limiting ideas, the *both/and* form invites participation. When differences are valued, the potential for argument is diminished. Conversations can be creative and yield valuable insight. This is a chance for us to explore ideas and try something on to see how it feels without carving laws into stone. *Exploring* rather than *expounding* creates space for thoughtful consideration, perhaps changing our mind, perhaps holding our ground, or perhaps experiencing a sudden insight that makes the current question irrelevant.

> Have a mind that is open to everything
> and attached to nothing.
>
> ~Tilopa

The Mental Connection

It has been estimated that 90 percent of our behavior comes from our subconscious mind, the largely unfiltered reservoir of beliefs, attitudes, and behaviors of those around us. Most of our subconscious programming is written from birth to age seven. When those around us are open-minded, we are free to question everything and create our own picture of reality. However, when early programming is delivered in an overly authoritarian, fearful way, we hesitate and hold back.

As American psychiatrist Rudolf Dreikurs has been quoted, "Children are keen observers but poor interpreters." Developmentally they are unable to assume any perspective other than their own. So, whatever a child in their limited capacity thinks is true often becomes an ingrained belief about themselves, as well as others and the outside world. Even if an experience is not inherently damaging to the child, the child's interpretation may be all that's needed to create a negative belief. This is why none of us really makes it through childhood unscathed. By the time we reach adulthood, our deeply rooted beliefs operate on a subconscious level, driving what we do (or don't do) and what we say (or don't say).

When our childhood experiences are particularly painful or problematic, our core beliefs are distorted or negative. The degree to which they become distorted depends on the conditions of our experiences as well as factors such as age, temperament, genetic inheritance, and the support we received or failed to receive from others to help us cope with the difficulties. Even then, a traumatic childhood has an adverse effect on our emotional and physical health and behavior patterns. Understanding that our beliefs may be distorted due to negative childhood experiences puts the power of choice back in our hands. We can choose to become aware of what's driving us, discard it if it does not serve us, replace it with what does, and move forward with belief in our innate goodness and completeness.

We can release messages that don't align with our truth and make room for our own interpretations based on our experiences in the present. The subconscious mind has no time clock. Every age we've been has been recorded and can be accessed. It has big-picture wisdom. It guides the healing process, carefully untying the knots of confusion and choosing the memories that are ready to be healed. As the subconscious is cleared of negative conditioning, its creative nature emerges. It becomes a powerful tool for building new programs that get us where we want to go.

A CONNECTED HEART AND MIND

Our heart and mind are meant to work together. When we are detached from our heart, the mind resists change. The mind identifies with our beliefs, and without the guidance of the heart, it becomes fearful and defensive, and when it is questioned, it goes into lockdown. Change originates in the heart, and the heart literally teaches the mind. The nature of our heart is love, and love has no past, present, or future; it simply is. As our heart creates new beliefs based in love and respect, our emotions update, and our mind relaxes. Our personal truth overwrites the old lies, and bonds of relationship strengthen. We create a deeper, truer relationship within us that is reflected into our relations with others.

As we learn how our mind and conditioning work, our natural curiosity returns. When we can't help but wonder, *What would it be like if I didn't react that way?* our creativity comes to its feet and applauds. We can imagine our transformed future in present time and feel the feelings and emotions of our healed state going forward. Curiosity isn't easily stopped; throughout the day, you find yourself wondering, *What it would be like if*... and, at that moment, you are further unbound to the problem; you are writing a new story, and your mind and body feel it. A curious mind and an active imagination are strong medicine. They move you along the healing path and toward whatever goal you set.

The Physical Connection

While it's true that early childhood experiences have a profound and long-lasting influence on us at all levels, we *can* heal. We can reclaim the health of our natural condition. Freed from the weight of negative conditioning, we have the ability and energy to maintain our health, increasing the length and quality of our lives. Dr. Bruce Lipton is one of a growing number of scientists who believe that DNA can be affected by our beliefs. He says, "The moment we change our perception is the moment we rewrite the chemistry of our body." Putting Lipton's statement into practice is a choice we can make.

We come into the world carrying our family's *epigenetic* imprint encoded in our genes. Epigenetic refers to external influences on the expression of our genes. Family patterns are tagged in our genetic code and can be activated or left inactive depending on what goes on around us. Epigenetics isn't the whole story. While the family patterns we inherit influence the choices we make and the experiences we have, they do not define us or set us on a course that can't be altered. The great equalizer to what could be a rigged game is *brain plasticity*.

We have the creativity to rise above our genetics, have new ideas, and change our beliefs throughout life. The old understanding was that we were hard wired in our early twenties and that was that—our fate was sealed. The new understanding of how the brain works holds the door open for making changes throughout life. We can grow new neural structures that will hold new beliefs and choose behaviors that reflect those beliefs. This is what we mean by authenticity. We become the authors of our own lives.

The Spirit Connection

Life is a fabric of energy and light. From the strands of our DNA to the infinite possibilities of our next moment's experience, we live in relation to many levels of awareness, feeling, thought, perception, memory, and identity. All the aspects that make us human beings are constantly interacting. To think of our mind, body, and spirit as separate creates a kind of schizophrenia: a deeply buried, barely remembered knowledge of wholeness, and an experience of great loss and emptiness. We are heir to *all* levels of consciousness—the highest being connection to spirit. *Spirit* refers to the very essence of life, the active consciousness that flows throughout everything in the universe.

Everything in our universe is a form of energy and is influenced by all levels of consciousness. Our beliefs affect what takes place in our body, and we get stuck when there is an imbalance in the flow of energy that sustains our spirit. We lose conscious connection, and *"the still small voice within"* falls silent. We become overly reliant on the voices of our culture. Whether it is an advertisement for a faster car or smoother bourbon, or the pursuit of more degrees, fame and fortune, or the drug dealer on the corner, we'll use almost anything to fill the void, that "hole in our soul." We medicate and teeter between anxiety and depression, always on the edge, never quite comfortable, always trying to prove we are good enough.

The more uncomfortable we become, the greater the *dis-ease* and the more likely we are to seek refuge from the feelings of not enough — not good enough, not smart enough, not cool enough, not pretty, thin, or strong enough. When we add on top of that the dysfunctional nature of our collective culture — the anger, injustice, constant judgment, prejudice, crime, abuse, rape, sexual abuse, abandonment, rage, victim's mentality, and resentment — is there any wonder why we seek out ways to medicate our experience in this world? We make the ways of the world more important than the spirit of God's creation as authentic human beings. Remember, society clings to its desperate need to be "right," and we cling to our stories of "right" to remain a member in good standing of our family and community. All that aside, we can reclaim a life lived from our heart place and know ourselves as good enough and reclaim faith in ourselves and, above all, rekindle our relationship with spirit.

The limiting beliefs that keep us from spirit yield to the heart's imagination, creativity, and the courage to make that grand leap into transcendence. Nothing can keep us from our true destiny when we firmly claim it. It is by no mere coincidence that catastrophic chaos signals the opportunity for transformation. Whether it is an addiction, an obsessive behavior, a painful experience, or anything else that keeps us from experiencing our wholeness, *our wholeness is our birthright*. Whatever is blocking us from the fullness of life and of our own fulfillment bows down to the truth of who we are in our heart and soul. Reclaiming ourselves and living the expression of our personal truth is the spirit of Heart Reconnection.

IT'S THE EXPERIENCE
OF BEING HUMAN

We've all had good days and bad days. We've all made terrible choices, great choices, and some okay choices. At some point, we've all been honorable, and at other times, we've all been dishonorable. This is the experience of living life as a human being. None of that changes the essence of who we are at our center. We are born of the light of creation, and we live life in this world, in our physical form, until our body dies and our spirit returns to the light. Our value in the eyes of the creator never changes; only our quality of life and experience in this world change according to the many variables we encounter here. We are spirit living as human; we are not the experiences we have here. As we discussed, over the course of our life, we lose connection to our true self and fall under the spell of our roles and beliefs. We take on stories as identities and behaviors as definitions of self. We cling to trying to be right so we can have a place in the world. We spin truth to fit the situation. The spinning starts at an early age, and unless we are fortunate enough to have life intervene, we might never stop spinning—therein is the blessing and the curse.

Living from the Heart

And now here is my secret, a very simple secret:
It is only with the heart that one can see rightly;
what is essential is invisible to the eye.

~Antoine de Saint-Exupéry,
The Little Prince

L iving to please others at the expense of our own authenticity is a recipe for trouble, but living life only to please ourselves is also a problem. Living from the heart brings balance; it assures our own well-being and is the source of empathy and compassion for others. Balance isn't necessarily a 50-50 split. The heart—not the mind—holds our innate fairness. The mind is subject to conditioning, but the heart holds the truth of who we are. The mind can "forget to forget," and it can hang on to judgments, fears, scorecards, and resentments for a very long time, whether it's a thought pattern, an old habit, a grudge, or that worn-out sweatshirt. The heart holds the power to forgive or let go, freeing us to move on.

Transformation Is a Lifelong Ability

We have an inborn ability to transform ourselves. We can replace harsh judgment with discernment. We can practice decision-making that flows from the heart to the head. We can choose to be open to new information in light of what we know to be true. We can suspend prejudgment pending further investigation rather than automatically rejecting new ideas or being overly influenced by them. Guided by our heart, our brain builds new neural pathways to hold our discoveries.

There's a caveat: even though we have awakened to our soul's original connection with the universe and are feeling loved, accepted, and whole, the world has not given up on getting us back. Indigenous stories wisely include a trickster, reminding us to be aware. Life can be compelling and seductive in its efforts. It is far wiser to be alert and watchful than naive and fearful.

Like characters in a play, we develop a cast of personalities that we can shift in and out of depending on whom we are with and where we are hanging out. Over time, we lose our awareness of our true self and drift further away from our heart. This is the disconnection we seek to heal. We can honor our truth that is born inside us. We can choose to believe in ourselves.

There is nothing wrong with worldly riches, position, success, or the pursuit of those things; thinking that the world is bad is outdated thinking. However, living excessively and sometimes exclusively from material consciousness leaves us out of balance and at risk of becoming deaf to the wisdom of our own true self. We can fall under the spell of our personality with all its quirks, fears, and temptations. We can gain fame and fortune but end up uncomfortable in our own skin. We may meet all the requirements of the world's rules for success, but still feel disconnected and lost, not even knowing why we feel so bad. When we have lost our connection to our heart, we have lost the true source of peace, and we slide closer to the edge of despair.

Paradoxically, that moment of despair can be the catalyst of a profound awakening if we don't submit to a quick fix or some other temporary distraction. We *can* heal what we have inherited. We *can* heal from the injuries we have received or inflicted on ourselves. We can allow the survival behaviors and practices to transform into talents and practices that can be of benefit to ourselves and others. We can release the energy of suffering and judgment. We can experience true self-worth. Once awakened, we can choose to live the life our heart desires for us. We have the option of reengaging our old life, or we can put our attention on developing our new one. We have a choice.

The Gift of Suffering

Life has its paradoxical moments; what first appears as a curse can turn out to be a true gift. Some call it hitting bottom; others call it grace. Or, as Alice Walker says in her book *The Temple of My Familiar,* "A heart breaks open." Our broken heart can be the opening through which we find our way back home. There is light on the other side of the suffering. We are called out to look into the mirror of time and life and question ourselves. We can look into our own eyes and see a new vision. With can find that glimmer of light reminding us that there was a time before all challenges and heartbreaks took over our life. We recall who we were before we sought refuge in the behaviors and ways of coping that now have us trapped.

Our capacity to heal is far greater than our suffering. As we step into our healing, we step into the light of self-awareness and the gifts of personal redemption that call up our spirit's greatest strengths. This is the hero's journey. It can be a tough one, but it is a journey for which we were created, and we have the resources we need to prevail.

The Heart's Journey

The heart's journey is a journey of reclaiming the gifts we abandoned long ago to fit into the world around us. It is a matter of realizing that we are who we are supposed to be, including the effects of the adventures and misadventures we've had. Wisdom comes from living the life that's in us. We can't find it by living someone else's life; we can't Google it or sign up for a course at the local college. It's found in the discoveries we make along the way, day by day, while remembering that we are whole, valuable, and loved.

Throughout this journey, remember, the world doesn't go away, and it doesn't give up the idea of getting us back into the matrix that got us where we are. We are always at risk of falling back into our old ways and losing sight of our gifts, particularly when making the transformational changes that shift our very frame of reference. We are vulnerable while we create the new brain structures to hold our transformation. This is the difference between body and spirit. Spirit "gets" it; in fact, it never lost it. It takes the body time to build the place for transformation to live. This is the energetic space between two worlds, the threshold between ambiguity and clarity; a no man's land. We must remain steadfast on our journey, and allow the heart to take the lead.

Moving Forward

We are taught that following the leader will lead us to happiness, security, and fulfillment, and in this way, our cultural programming has created fear of the unknown. Stepping out of our familiar patterns is scary, precisely because we've been taught to believe that anything outside of what's familiar is potentially harmful. This is the line in the sand, so to speak, that gives community its power. We have a human need for validation that we are on the right track. Once we cross that threshold into the unknown, going back to the "old familiar" begins to lose its charm. Remember Wild Heart's theory from earlier in the book? She reminds us that creativity trumps conditioning. When we reinforce our new thinking, our new brain structures get stronger.

Moving forward despite the discomfort and fear is how we reinforce our belief in our true self. We connect with the deep abiding courage of our heart, and we build trust in ourselves that is stronger than the past. It is said that in the world of spirit, everything happens at the same time, but in the physical world, there's a time gap between placing our order and the arrival of the pizza truck in the driveway. In the physical realm, we need to keep stepping forward to eventually experience our new reality. We do that by creating a practice or belonging to a community that reminds us of where we are going, keeping us focused on the new world.

JOURNALING:
SNAPSHOTS ON THE PATH

You are standing on the edge of a life-changing course of events in which you are the main character in your story. Throughout this journey, you are discovering aspects of yourself that can easily slip through the cracks of consciousness. During the process of transformation, it's an excellent idea to keep a journal to jot down your reflections. It doesn't matter if you're a good writer or even if you write in complete sentences; the simple act of taking notes on where you are in your process is important as you journey forward. Insight branches—it keeps sprouting new ideas and growing. Your journal provides a striking picture of your journey, a place to remember where you've been while reinforcing how far you've come. You will get the most out of your journey if you make a blank book your companion and fill it with all the wonders of your experiences, questions, reflections, and thoughts.

While a lot can be said on the subject, the journey ahead cannot be accurately described in words. It is an experience that reveals itself to each of us on a personal level as we navigate the path. We are in a living engagement with life as individuals and also as a group, an expedition through our history, our present, and our future. It can restore our sense of self when it has strayed, bringing it back into alignment with our spirit's idea of who we are. There are no wrong answers and no hidden agendas in this process. Our answers are within, or perhaps more accurately, we *are* the answer.

CHAPTER

4

Letting Go of Illusions

It takes courage to grow up and become who you really are.

~E. E. Cummings

Spiritual teachers from every tradition agree that awakening to the true self begins with the question, *Who am I?* The truth isn't what other people have told us we are, it isn't what we wish we were, and it might not even be whom we think or believe we are. It is simply, and grandly what we *really* are. This begins the journey letting go of beliefs and illusions we have wrapped ourselves in and depending on spirit.

In *The Spirit Recovery Meditation Journal,* Lee McCormick asks this question of himself. He writes, "Who am I, really? I've tried for so long to be who or what I thought people wanted or told me to be that

I don't want to do that again. I don't want to be defined by the world around me. To not be sure of who I think I am is really scary. In fact, my question of identity has me hanging out over a deep black void. 'Keep coming back.' Those are gentle words of support whispered in my ear. The journey is not easy. That I have strayed so far from my truth is sad, but it's all going to work out if I keep showing up for myself."

As Lee's reflection illustrates, when we ask this question of ourselves, we may not have the answer, and that can feel frightening. We might want to grab the first thing that comes to mind to comfort or assure ourselves. However, much of what we have come to believe about ourselves needs to be chiseled away from our outer layers before we can recognize our personal truth without preconceptions and judgments. This takes time, and we return to the question and to ourselves again and again.

Who we are might be revealed to us slowly, in layers. When we settle into ourselves and trust the heart's way, we can appreciate the pace at which we are moving. The well-known axiom "More shall be revealed" seems to fit a lot of life as well as our ever-evolving understanding of our true self. "Keep coming back, indeed!" Reconnecting with our heart is simply showing up for ourselves again and again in a process of revelation.

X

YOU ARE HERE

No matter the challenges and troubles you've encountered, they have brought you to this moment in time at this exact place exactly as you are. The *how you got here* part of the story transforms into wisdom—life lessons learned through experience. Self-defeating behaviors steal hopes and dreams, and then come back to steal your sense of self. You risk losing touch with everything you once held in high esteem and those you hold dear. Behaviors that block you from the life you want to live separate you from your self—from your own true heart. No matter how far you think you have strayed, you are always *right here.* Your heart waits for you to realize that you are *right here.* You're in the perfect time and place no matter where X marks the spot.

Triggers and Reactive Patterns

What we might consider a great life comes about through an alchemy of self-reflection, choices, and how well we mind and direct our attention and practice. When we live in fear and suffering, our attention tends to be hooked by the emotions related to our suffering, such as sadness, anxiety, anger, and doubt, and these feelings tend to become old familiar companions in life. As we become more familiar and used to the feelings that arise when our attention goes into stories of suffering or trauma or fear, whatever stories that run repetitively through our mind, we trigger an emotional reaction or response to those stories. (You may have heard these repetitive cycles referred to as "brain loops.")

Energetically, we develop an appetite for the frequency of emotions that are familiar to us. People who experience rage have created an appetite for the energy of rage. This appetite is not unlike a drug in its frequency and false sense of empowerment. The same can be said of living with sadness or having grown up in a home that had an overlay of any prevalent emotional frequency. We tend to recreate what has become familiar to us. Even when what's familiar was miserable, it still feels "safe" to us in a sense precisely because it's familiar. Our mind naturally gives attention to the familiar, which feeds that pattern and reinforces that energy and emotional reaction.

This is a cause-and-effect scenario. Our mind runs an old story that's possibly been triggered by a current experience, and the present experience calls up the energy of the old story that's been stored in our emotional body, which does not know the difference between what is real in the present moment and an old mind-tale memory of heartbreak, trauma, or suffering. The emotions come up, driven by the combination of past and present experiences.

This is the dynamic that creates reactions in the moment that are out of proportion to the present situation. We overreact. It is a setup that we have no conscious awareness of, and it owns us. Being creatures of habit, we tend to follow our patterns. We tend to "believe" our patterns as truth and reality. When there is no conscious awareness of where or what we are giving our attention to in our thoughts, these feelings feed into our patterns, reinforcing them, giving them life, and ultimately giving the thoughts, beliefs, and subsequent emotional reactions power over us in the moment. While the emotions are true, the beliefs and thoughts that trigger those emotional reactions may not be true at all in this moment, but until we have intentionally questioned our beliefs, thoughts, and stories, we will keep falling into the emotional "rabbit hole" of our familiar story that opens every time we get triggered.

Paying Attention and Asking Questions

The practice of asking, "Where is my attention?" is the key to breaking these reactive patterns. This is not a practice of judgment. There is no "right" or "wrong" to be defended or supported here. This is a simple questioning of, "Is that really true? Does this belief exist here and now in my reality? What is the story I am telling myself?" As we question, we bring our attention into the moment, and from an observer's point of view, we are able to hold a place of awareness with ourselves.

The wisdom of our heart can be revealed once we shift our attention from the judgmental and reasoning nature of our mind and toward the witness and compassion of the heart's awareness. We can see that much of our suffering is the result of our unconscious patterns and stories and their subsequent emotional reactions running on automatic pilot through our mind. All we need to do is step back and ask the question, "Is that true?" Then, we sit with the answers that come and learn to practice breaking the patterns of thought, action, and reaction that we have created without knowing any better. There is no need or benefit to explaining or justifying; the answer is a simple yes or no. With gratitude and compassion, we can question all aspects of our lives for the sake of being 100 percent responsible for our own experience and choices. This is an act of freedom and power.

Awareness of where, what, and why we are giving attention to any thought or belief is a great gift we can give to ourselves. Practice makes the master, and the master knows their art. Each of us is living the artistry of our life's creation. Isn't it amazing that, by owning our place in time, our attention, and our ability to question and choose from where we will listen for responses to our questions, we can re-create our way of living from the inside out? We are the light, not the shadows we cast, yet many of us have learned to live for the shadow and have lost relationship to the light. By the practice of attention, we will awaken to our personal truth and our greatest opportunities to create a life we love waking up to in the morning.

Gaining Awareness Through Practice

Reconnecting to our heart is not an event; it's a practice. Approaching the practice with childlike curiosity, we unleash our imagination, and all things are possible. The mind is not the enemy, but without the guidance and grounding of the heart, the mind wanders, plans, ruminates, frets, and obsesses in an attempt to keep us safe, comfortable, and validated.

We are conditioned to live in our mind and rely on facts as our only means of knowing. When we have a feeling we'd rather not have, we tend to try to think our way through it to resolve it while completely bypassing the wisest part of ourselves that could give the mind some guidance. The mind is then at a disadvantage and does the only thing it knows how to do: *think in circles*. This can be exhausting, and the only way out, it seems, is checking out. But there's a much better way.

Our heart is positioned between the head where the voices of culture echo and the gut where our emotions are felt. With practice, we can teach our mind to not react to the fear in our gut and choose instead the wise counsel of our heart. Inner truth reveals itself through feelings and intuition. It takes time and practice to learn the language of the heart, and of course the mind is still going to claim to know it all. No matter how demanding or noisy it might become up there in our head, we have the power to shift our attention to that deeper place within where we discover the miracle of being our true self.

We *can* provide the mind with the guidance to allow us to a lead a life of freedom and joy. This level of internal connection, "mastery over the mind," is spoken of in all the Great Mystery schools, often at great length. It comes through mind shifting and practicing stillness.

How to Mind Shift

A healthy balanced mind is naturally curious; it investigates and makes sense of things. The unbalanced mind wanders aimlessly; it can be critical and judgmental of anything it perceives. Mind shifting is consciously shifting your attention away from those old loops of critical, judgmental, negative thoughts that block your path or lead you in a direction you don't want to go. It is as simple as becoming aware in the moment that your mind has wandered down an old beaten path and taking a deep breath as you gently shift your attention away from your mind's commentary and follow your breath back into the heart.

Avoid arguing with your mind (it will give you a hard time) and gently return to your breath and your heart again and again. Through repeated practice of witnessing the mind and *shifting* back to "heart awareness," you are reshaping your thinking and reconnecting to your spiritual power. Remember, awareness and attention allow you to intervene before you react out of habit. You will find a less demanding, quieter voice that is encouraging along your journey toward a full, free life.

How to Practice Stillness

Stillness simply means intentionally doing nothing with the mind, letting it chatter without paying any attention to it, and it quiets. Meditation is a stillness practice. The Heart Reconnection Meditation script on pages 30–32 is designed to help you communicate with your heart. It can strengthen your connection with your heart and awaken your awareness of your inner life. The more frequently you do this meditation, the more familiar it will become, the deeper into the process you will go, and the more awareness of your internal life you will gain.

It's difficult, if not impossible, to both read and meditate at the same time, so it's a good idea to make an audio recording of the script. Pause for a few moments or more between the statements to allow yourself or another listener ample time to follow the suggestions. As with any advice you receive, you can simply follow the suggestions in the script that personally feel good to you and/or change the language to something that resonates better.

HEART RECONNECTION
MEDITATION SCRIPT

Lie on a blanket or sit on a chair or couch—whatever feels right and comfortable to you.

Draw your breath in slowly, taking it all the way down into your belly, and feel yourself expanding as the breath fills you. Hold your breath for a few seconds and then release it slowly, feeling your muscles soften and releasing any stress. (Repeat for six breaths.)

Return to your naturally comfortable breathing rhythm and close your eyes. Imagine that you are in one of your favorite places in nature; it can be a real place or one you make up.

⚹ *Notice the colors around you.*
⚹ *Notice the sounds you hear.*
⚹ *Notice the temperature of the air on your skin.*
⚹ *Notice the time of day or night.*
⚹ *Notice what it feels like to be in that place.*

Now, in your imagination, find a spot where you can sit comfortably in that place—a chair, a blanket on the ground, on a warm rock, against a tree. Relax.

You might notice a younger version of yourself playing nearby. Time is not linear in the subconscious mind. You can be your adult self and your child self at the same time.

Breathe deeply now and allow yourself to relax even more . . . feeling more relaxed . . . more relaxed.

If you would like to communicate with your heart, place a hand over your heart and imagine breathing into this sacred space. Take three more breaths into your heart. Imagine your heart responding to the breath and notice how it feels.

✕ *Is your heart a color?*

✕ *Is your heart pumping?*

✕ *Can you hear the sound it makes?*

✕ *How do you feel?*

Take a moment to appreciate your heart's faithfulness. It pumps day and night…day and night…day and night.

In your own words, let your heart know you appreciate it, keeping you alive through all the good times…and all the rough times.

Ask your heart what it needs from you. Is it something you can say yes to?

Ask your heart for what you need. Do you need to feel more love? Do you need to give love more? Is there anything else you want to ask of your heart? Go ahead and ask now.

Relax and notice how it feels to communicate with your heart, the very organ that keeps you alive.

In a few moments, you will come back to your awakened consciousness. For now, just experience this connection and realize that you can have a talk with your heart anytime, anyplace, about anything.

Feel gratitude in your heart for your heart and breathe into it.

Feel your heart glowing and pumping and feel gratitude pulsing throughout your whole body. Remember, your heart loves you. You can spend time aware of your heart whenever you want to.

As you anticipate awakening, you can bring with you anything that was helpful and leave behind anything you don't need and allow it to disappear from your mind.

Slowly bring your attention back into this room, knowing you can return anytime.

(Slightly increase the volume of your voice.)

Start becoming aware of the sounds around you.

When you are ready, open your eyes. Sit quietly for a few moments to fully make the transition from your inner world to where you are now. When you feel like you are ready, you can make notes in your journal.

Journal Prompts:

- ✖ What was important to you about this experience?
- ✖ How did it feel to connect with your heart–spirit?
- ✖ What did you say to your heart?
- ✖ What did you receive from your heart?
- ✖ Free write anything that comes to mind.

✖

Wherever we are starting from, we can only start from the beginning. We bring with us all our past experiences…everything we have inherited…all of our beliefs and perceived truths…our judgments of ourselves, others, and the world…our hopes and dreams…our disappointments and pain. We set off with a heavy load, a load that weighs us down, a load that we try so hard to pretend isn't on our back. But now we do so with the intention of bringing awareness to what we're carrying around, reducing the weight of our burden by letting go of what does not serve us, and cutting the ties that pull us in the opposite direction. We forge ahead on the Heart Reconnection path, the path of the medicine wheel.

CHAPTER 5

Embarking on the Path of the Wheel

When you know who you are;
when your mission is clear and you burn
with the inner fire of unbreakable will;
no cold can touch your heart;
no deluge can dampen your purpose.
You know that you are alive.

—Chief Seattle

ertain experiences in life tend to come around again and again—not necessarily in a negative way but in a predict-able way, like the seasons of the year. Circle teachings such as medicine wheels, mandalas, and labyrinths have been used around the world to evoke spiritual insights and healing since the dawn of humanity. The medicine wheel is perhaps better known among indigenous cultures as the sacred hoop of life or the great circle of life. Circle teachings are based in universal spiritual principles such as love, compassion, gratitude, forgiveness, generosity, honesty, courage, and wisdom. They honor all paths. The wisdom they hold has been chanted, danced, drummed, and applied to life for many thousands of years. Its roots go deep into the heart of the earth.

Acceptance Begins the Journey Home

Medicine wheel practices reveal to us how our experiences of life contribute to us being exactly who we are in such a way that we cannot deny the sheer truth of it; we cannot escape ourselves. In that moment of grace, we are offered nonjudgmental acceptance, a moment of truth that begins the journey home. Acceptance does not simply mean satisfaction with where we are but that we are no longer fighting with ourselves about it. In the reality of the moment, truth frees us to move ahead into the life that better reflects who we are. When we blame ourselves for our poor choices, we are feeding negativity. Acceptance is a spiritual awakening, a new consciousness, and we can actually feel our mind open, and the light shine in. Hope returns, and we feel like we're going to make it. This is the experience of the miracle of transformation, and that's just the beginning of the journey! Acceptance opens the way for learning how to love. *Teach me how to love myself* is a perfect starting prayer.

What's Ahead?

The wheel offers guidance to all who seek to find their true self and live a life of purpose. Spending time on the wheel helps us discover our personal truth while gaining insight and wisdom about life and the world throughout the process.

The wheel symbolizes the life journey we are walking together as communities as well as our personal life journey. It helps us discover new things about ourselves and about life and also helps us remember things we may have forgotten that will help us on our journey. It offers a place to reflect on life and to realize what we most value about ourselves, what we want to develop, what we can contribute to our family and friends, and what we would like to leave behind. The wheel is not bound by time. We can walk it many times and receive new insights and gifts appropriate to the challenges and questions we bring to it, no matter where we are on the journey.

Each time we look at our reflection in the wheel, we are seeing ourselves and life from where we are now, in this moment. Every day is a new day. Every experience passes through us, giving us new insights, inspirations, challenges, gifts, heartbreaks, and so on. We are like the river, never the same person from one day to the next; as we learn, shift, grow, and evolve, our perspectives also shift. When we enter into a process of deep healing work, we show up like the windshield on a car after a long drive through life, covered in mud, dirt, splattered bugs, raindrops—you name it. It's all that stuff that has collected throughout our life's experience that we never cleaned off. Our view of the world and our understanding of ourselves are filtered through this windshield of life.

There's no need to judge our "windshield" or the process that got it this way; it is what it is. What's important here is that we *can* clean our windshield. By stepping into our Heart Reconnection practices, we come to terms with all the stories, heartbreaks, opinions, fears, agreements, judgments, and so on that are smeared across our windshield. As is so often the case, this is a blessing and curse. The gift of recognizing the dirty windshield is an invitation to learn how to clean it and keep it clear. If not for the struggles and pain of life, we might never have realized that we had collected all that stuff on our window of perception during our journey; we might never have slowed down long enough to see our true self and life from a clear perceptive. This doesn't mean we aren't still suffering, uncomfortable, and challenged—that's the curse of sorts. However, when we step into it all, we bring the light of our awareness to bear and all the grace and power of our heart to make choices that will reframe our lives, ourselves, and our future.

The Dance of Healing

The medicine wheel is the perfect circle for reflection, allowing us to come back again and again to those aspects of ourselves that we need to reclaim and rebalance. This is the dance of healing. Each time we come to the circle to sit with an aspect or experience of being human, we bring who we are in this moment with us. As we grow and learn, our point of view shifts. Our ability to understand expands. We come to realize that we can heal and outgrow old stories and traumas. We can undo and release old behaviors, addictions, and attachments.

Of course this takes time and many passes around the wheel. This is challenging to our mind, which demands results now. At the same time, it offers us the gift of developing patience and determination to hang in there because we can see clearly enough to truly believe that we are worth it.

Isn't it funny how we keep finding ourselves in the blessing/curse place where we hold the key to what we will make of each challenge and opportunity? It is up to us. Want to suffer and make it all so hard? Okay, it can be. Want to learn to relax, breathe deeply, and not take everything so personally or seriously? Well then, the experience can be intriguing and rewarding.

By walking the way of the wheel, we are rising up as we work on ourselves. Literally, we "lighten" up. Letting go of old baggage, we allow more light from within to shine into the world around us. It is amazing the gifts that life offers us when we are willing to say yes to reclaiming our truth and step into the center of our being on our journey around the medicine wheel.

The Circle and Four Directions

In its physical form, a medicine wheel is a circle divided evenly into four quadrants, each quadrant represents one of the four cardinal directions—east, south, west, and north—symbolizing our life journey.

Before we begin our journey within, we view the entirety of the medicine wheel—where we stand in the center of the circle and experience our heart from the inside. We experience our living, beating connection to the cosmos and all that resides there. We ask for the realization that we are loved and whole and are part of the Great Mystery and web of life. We ask for compassion, love, and creativity to flow from our heart.

We begin our journey around the wheel in the **east** where the morning sun brings light into the day and where our spirit light first enters the world as an infant. As we connect with our newborn spirit, we might remember this young character's hopes and dreams.

We then travel to the **south**, where we meet ourselves as adults. We reflect on our past and current relationships with others. We learn important relationship skills and have the chance to transform family patterns that we no longer wish to participate in.

Next, we visit the **west** and meet our shadow selves—those parts of us that we have kept hidden. Shadow has much to share with us; it deepens us, adding dimension to our self-understanding.

We then go to the **north**, where we claim our wisdom—what we have learned from our journey around the wheel and the changes we have made. We dream a dream for ourselves and our hopes for the community, and the world.

The Heart of the Practice, the Heart of the Wheel

The beauty of working within a medicine wheel is its ability to hold meanings that uniquely work for each of us. There are many traditions and many meanings assigned to each direction. The values, aspects of character, elements—these are all flexible from tradition to tradition. The presentation of the medicine wheel in this book is just one way to take this journey. This is a personal experience for each of us, so there's no need to get caught up in defining exactly how this process should play out for us or get stuck on "The east means this, and the south means that." Each direction means many things in different situations to different people, and none of them are more correct than others. What's actually important here aren't the qualities assigned to a particular direction but when and how those qualities apply to us individually in our own life, our own process, and our own experience.

Flexibility is a gift in life. Each of us can honor our own traditions, beliefs, and experiences as we travel the wheel, while allowing it to assist us in this experience. The wheel is a road map, a tool, that guides us along our journey of awakening, healing, and Heart Reconnection. The form of the tool is not more important than the outcome of the experience.

To use this tool, some of us might want to jump in with both feet and see what happens; others might want a little guidance. For those who like instructions, here's a suggestion: read or reread one of the upcoming chapters and then just sit with whatever is going on for you. Reflect on your position on the wheel or consider how what you read does or doesn't resonate with you. Explore your inner landscape by trying out the exploration exercises presented and journaling your insights and questions.

The way we will come to know ourselves and get to the heart of our personal truth is to spend time with ourselves. That's what the medicine wheel is all about. We simply need to set aside time for ourselves several times a week to just hang out with what is.

※

It is important to set your intention when approaching a spiritual practice. We are suggesting that this first trip around the wheel is for the purpose of gaining a sense of your true self. Are you ready to carry your question on your journey, asking, "Who am I?" Are you willing to go to the center of your being to the true, authentic you—the person you wish to be, were meant to be, and who already are in your heart? If so, turn the page and step up.

CHAPTER

6

East: Entering the Wheel

Beautiful you rise, O eternal living god.
You are radiant, lovely, powerful.
Your love is great, all-encompassing.
Your rays make all radiant,
Your brightness gives life to hearts!

~Egyptian Prayer of Praise
(1550–1305 B.C.E.)

Time of life:	Birth, Childhood, and Early Teen
Time of year:	Spring
Time of day:	Daybreak
Qualities:	Love, innocence, hope, playfulness, curiosity, imagi-nation, creativity, trust, openness, vulnerability, joy
Spirit animal:	Eagle
Color:	Yellow
Embodiment:	Heart
Phrase:	Earth, My Body

The first light of day comes out of the east, and it is out of the east that our spirit light comes into human form. East is the place of possibilities and opportunities—the source of imagination, creativity, and openheartedness. East represents all new beginnings: birth, childhood, entrance into adolescence, awakening of creativity, initiating new beliefs and behaviors, and more. East awakens us to the divine light within us.

Eagle is the spirit guide of the east. The Eagle is the one who can see from the smallest detail while having the ability to also step back and look out across the whole horizon. Eagle is a warrior in spirit and a fierce loving protector of her young. Eagle flies high and far. The power of Eagle supports us in looking at the details of our life's experience, realizing all we have experienced and, at the same time, rising above to look across our whole horizon of possibilities. We see both what we need to tend to, address, and heal. Looking up and out, we realize we hold the ability to dream a new life, a greater relationship to life and spirit. Eagle carries strong medicine. She carries wisdom, strength, and healing. Eagle is the master of awareness and vision.

In this healing journey, we begin at the beginning, so we return to our place as children. With the qualities of Eagle, we can move from deep within to the greater open awareness of all potential and possibilities available once we have cleaned and cleared our present moment reality.

Child Heart's Spirit

The child holds our survival instinct and our ability to heal; it is our life force that refuses to give up on us regardless of the circumstances. There are times when life becomes overwhelming; we instinctively detach from those situations, and our memory of them fades. In this life-saving disconnection, we can also lose awareness of our sacred nature and the gifts of our child spirit, qualities such as innocence, willingness to forgive, unconditional love, and curiosity. We can be left with vague troubling impressions that something went wrong, that something is missing, but without full access to the memories. These feelings haunt us, and we assume it's about something we did or didn't do. While we continue to grow and develop in many ways, we are held back in others: our sense of self-worth is marginal, and issues of dependency can mean being overly invested in pleasing others rather than coming from within. Or we might close down and ignore all advice from others. Our confidence can be shaky or boastful; we have issues with authority figures. In short, we are not getting the full benefit of being us.

In her seminal work *Adult Children of Alcoholics*, Janet Geringer Woititz, EdD, identified thirteen characteristics commonly found among adults who grew up in homes where alcoholic disruption ruled. These characteristics are now considered to be common in dysfunctional families, regardless of the causes of the chaos. Our cultural understanding of what constitutes dysfunctional is broadening as well. As you review the list below, notice those that resonate with you and pause for a moment in recognition of your journey. It isn't necessary to have all the characteristics to indicate a troubled childhood, nor is having one or two definitive of one.

1. Adult children of alcoholics guess at what normal behavior is.
2. Adult children of alcoholics have difficulty following a project through from beginning to end.
3. Adult children of alcoholics lie when it would be just as easy to tell the truth.
4. Adult children of alcoholics judge themselves without mercy.
5. Adult children of alcoholics have difficulty having fun.
6. Adult children of alcoholics take themselves very seriously.
7. Adult children of alcoholics have difficulty with intimate relationships.
8. Adult children of alcoholics overreact to changes over which they have no control.
9. Adult children of alcoholics constantly seek approval and affirmation.
10. Adult children of alcoholics usually feel that they are different from other people.
11. Adult children of alcoholics are super responsible or super irresponsible.
12. Adult children of alcoholics are extremely loyal, even in the face of evidence that the loyalty is undeserved.
13. Adult children of alcoholics are impulsive. They tend to lock themselves into a course of action without giving serious consideration to alternative behaviors or possible

consequences. This impulsively leads to confusion, self-loathing, and loss of control over their environment. In addition, they spend an excessive amount of energy cleaning up the mess.[2]

Childhood: Vulnerability and Power

We think of newborns as all soft and cuddly, which they are of course, but we tend to forget the power of the child's spirit. Here, pediatrician and psychoanalyst Dr. Donald Woods Winnicott reminds us of the child's tenacity and strength:

> What is a normal child like? Does he just eat and grow and smile sweetly? No, that is not what he is like. The normal child, if he has confidence in mother and father, pulls out all the stops. In the course of time, he tries out his power to disrupt, to destroy, to frighten, to wear down, to waste, to wangle, and to appropriate. At the start, he absolutely needs to live in a circle of love and strength (with consequent tolerance) if he is not to be too fearful of his own thoughts and of his imaginings to make progress in his emotional development.

If we do not grow up in a circle of love and strength, our child spirit suffers. We may try to ignore the child as we grow, but the child never goes away. A tree is a good metaphor here. The center of the tree is called the heart, and each ring inside the tree carries nature's record of that year. As we grow, we incorporate the child, and like the rings of the tree, the child carries our history.

2 Woititz, Janet Geringer. "13 Characteristics." *Adult Children of Alcoholics*. Pompano Beach, FL: Health Communications, 1983. N. pag. Print. Used with permission.

Those lost aspects of our soul live in the shadow of our subconscious mind, influencing everything we think or do, how we interpret our world, how we respond to challenges, the choices we make, and how we make them. In a hand-behind-the-curtain way, the child is running the show! When we look beyond our early conditioning, we find the sacred innocence of the child within along with our fierce will to live. Healing begins when we realize that the child is safe in our heart, whole and perfect, waiting for us to come home.

NATURE IS ON OUR SIDE

Nature wants us to survive even in the face of overwhelming circumstances. We instinctively distance ourselves from the full impact of traumatic injuries until we get to a place in life where we can heal them. Healing begins as we reconnect with our heart and return to living in the flow of life again. We often assume that healing depends on knowing every aspect of our story. We try to figure it out as if figuring it out heals us. That is a logical assumption of the mind. However, healing happens in the heart, and the heart has its own intuitive, nonlinear way of conducting business. Our essential aspects (mind, body, and spirit) are meant to work together. Healing in the heart's way brings all aspects into a new more harmonious relationship with one another.

The Creativity of Healing

In the worldview of separation, we divided the two hemispheres of the brain, associating the right hemisphere with creativity and left hemisphere with analytical cognition. As it turns out, creativity involves a conversation between both hemispheres of the brain as well as the prefrontal cortex, our center of vision and higher order thinking, and an overall spirit of willingness working together in a cooperative venture.

The spirit of cooperative venture is the primary condition in which healing can occur and changes can be made, and it is the principle condition for transformation and all creative acts. Healing is a creative process, and it involves every aspect of our mind, body, and spirit working together. We imagine ourselves as the person we know in our heart that we are meant to be. We may underestimate ourselves at that point, but our higher self understands our commitment, and in time, we will be transformed into the person we are in our heart and soul.

Some of us might find that way of thinking inappropriate—that it says nothing about God's role in our lives. In the holistic worldview, there is no separation between the creator and creation; the divine dwells within us and within the cosmos. We suspect that the creator gave us the ability to heal ourselves and our ability to transcend difficulties, placing them in our heart and perhaps knowing that life was going to dish out some pretty difficult stuff.

Healing is not dependent on *knowing,* in the way of facts and figures. It is far more about believing in ourselves and in our right to be happy. A bit of 12-Step wisdom asks the question, *Do you want to be right or happy?* Of course, they are not mutually exclusive, but if we begin with the mind, we are starting on the wrong foot. The heart knows the way. It knows how to orchestrate balance and harmony in our body, mind, and spirit. We do not even need to know the details of how the heart comes up with the formulas. We just need to trust our heart with the job.

That doesn't mean we are idle passengers on the wellness journey. There are commonsense factors we can choose to practice that support healing, such as eating nourishing food in healthy portions, sleeping eight to ten hours a night, being a good neighbor, and having loving relations in our life. We'll take a closer look at those things and ways we can attend to them as we continue traversing the medicine wheel.

The Body's Book of Life

As you read earlier, our spirit arrives in our body unaware that it is carrying the genetic patterns of the lives of previous generations. Many indigenous traditions say that this energetic imprint of our ancestors reaches back seven generations. Imagine all that has been passed on to each of us from those who came before us, and how that binds the generations together through time and space for better or worse. Not only do we hold the opportunity to heal from our experiences in life, we also hold the power to heal our inherited bloodlines and release those behaviors, traumas that our ancestors never had the opportunity to address. As we give ourselves the gifts of healing, it is shared through time with those who came before us.

With so much stored in our physical body, it is no wonder that we get overwhelmed and come to feel so "heavy" in life. Isn't it interesting how we commonly call our story our "baggage"? Can you imagine how many suitcases it might require if we each had to pack up all our "stuff" and bring it with us every time we went anywhere?

Exploring the East

The main task we have when bringing the child into our awareness is to love it and take care of it. These practices are designed to help you in that process:

- ☙ Visualize what you loved to do when you were a child. What were your favorite games to play? What fascinated you? What were your dreams and fantasies? Set aside an afternoon to do something you liked to do when you were a child. For example, go to a park, swing on a swing, or walk barefoot in the grass. It will awaken the child within. Let your child guide you and show you what to do next.

- ☙ Place a photograph of yourself as a child where you can see it every day. If you don't have a photo, you can draw or paint a picture of yourself—stick figures count! Or use a drawing or image that reminds you of the childhood you should have had. Whenever you see the image throughout the day, say something positive such as "I see you. I love you. I am happy you are here with me." Keep it simple and straight from the heart!

- ☙ Choose a symbol to represent yourself as a child. The symbol can be something you find in nature, like a rock or shell or even a twig—or it can be something man-made like a marble, a small trinket, etc. Spend a few minutes simply holding it in your hand connecting with it. When you are ready, breathe into the symbol (literally, allow your breath to blow over it, visualizing your breath being absorbed by the object). Then hold it over your heart. Speak loving words or think thoughts that reflect love, such as "You are a great kid." Imagine how the child feels hearing those words. As you do this, notice what your mind is saying to you. Breathe deeply and replace any negative thoughts and mind shift away from them with loving words, even if it feels unnatural or as if it isn't true yet. When the mind and heart disagree, the heart will ultimately win if you stick with positive reinforcement. You are building a new neural pathway to connect you and your child. Transformation takes consistency and repetition of your affirmation. Keep it brief. When you say too much, you will slip back into your old story. Spend a few minutes each morning and evening breathing into the symbol of the healed child. Hold it over your heart, imagining how the child feels when you speak with love and respect in your voice.

BEING A
QUESTION CARRIER

East brings us the curiosity and open-heartedness to look at our life and the choices we made and imagine ourselves anew. It asks questions like, *Who am I? What are my hopes and dreams? Where am I going? What is my purpose?* You are just beginning this journey to self-awareness, and most likely you won't have answers to these life questions now, but it is important to ask them. This is a wisdom practice of being a question carrier. Wisdom has a way of finding us when we have ears to hear. Carrying a question creates openings for information and opportunities to reach us. It's unfortunate, but true, that education emphasizes answers, but life thrives on questions. As mentioned earlier, the path of enlightenment is paved with questions!

Healing the Whole Person

Healing the inner child is an exercise in putting first things first, paying attention to basics of life. Healthy eating and adequate sleep and loving relationships are needs that do not go away—ever. If we go without eating all day or eat only junk foods, we can easily lose our composure when things don't go exactly as we think they should; that's the presence of a neglected child making itself known. The same is true about our need for sleep. We also need friendships and mentoring and spending time with family members who are supportive of our healing.

You may be surprised by how challenging full-time caretaking of yourself can be! We'll focus on two of the basics, getting enough sleep and eating food that will sustain your body. Your commitment to self-care makes other commitments easier to keep.

A SELF-CARE COMMITMENT

Of course, it's possible to make a commitment without having a piece of paper to show for it, but we give form to our promise when we write it down. If you are ready and willing to take better care of yourself, your journal can be witness to this powerful step forward. It can also serve as an important reminder when you need one. You might simply write, "On this _____ day of _____, I commit to self-care" or it can be much more involved. Use whatever words you want to use to express your intention to truly care for yourself in all ways. Another idea is to choose a symbol to represent your self-care—maybe a shiny rock, a piece of wood, or a small figurine—and place it where you will see it every day. If it's small enough, you can even carry it in your pocket.

Healing is about creating something new out of the old—a fresh understanding of ourselves, a new awareness of our ability to turn neglect into good health and well-being by the choices we make. It's wise to be aware of what we are mindlessly putting into our bodies. Even mindlessness or the absence of choice is a choice. When you catch yourself tuning out, simply draw your attention to the fact that you are making conscious choices. This allows you to notice where you are out of balance and gives you an opportunity to make the healthy adjustments that will lead to clarity of mind and openness of heart and allow the light to come into your awareness.

We tend to avoid becoming aware of behaviors, beliefs, or thought processes when we think it means we have to change. When we are just beginning to build trust in ourselves, change is intimidating. It helps to separate these concepts: we can have awareness that we should make a change or even that we would like to make a change, and that we aren't ready to move ahead with it yet. In this case, we are in our personal truth, and truth is powerful. We can keep it on a to-do list in our journal or on a piece of paper kept nearby. We may need more time, and we may need more help to make the change, but the most important thing is to be honest with ourselves. A complete do over doesn't happen overnight and not even over the course of a year. But what we put on our list *will* happen in time because truth has a way of sticking around.

Change is the only constant in life. Change is happening every day whether we like it or not or can see it or not; life is a continuum of change. Awareness of the law of change allows us to use it in transforming our lives. Making a decision and setting your intention gives the energy of change direction. The universe is on our side; the old idea of us being pitted against nature was never true. We have self-determination. The art of transformation is in determining what we want out of the life's ever-changing nature.

REWIRING
SHORT-CIRCUITS

We are designed to learn from our experiences, and emotions play a big part in the conclusions we draw and the choices we make. Chaotic emotions block learning. Maladaptive coping behaviors short-circuit the natural process of experiencing, learning, and growing. They can affect our ability to think clearly, discern, and assimilate new information. In many cases, our coping behaviors began sometime during our childhood. Our wires

got overloaded and fizzled out, preventing us from making
new, healthy choices. We can create new circuits in the
present through self-care and practices that set us
back on the natural path of experiencing, learning,
and growing.

A Smorgasbord of Mysteries

It's easy to forget that teenagers are still children because they try
very hard to come across as mature and self-sufficient. Teens are in
the unique position of having one foot in childhood and the other
in adulthood. There's a smorgasbord of mysteries awaiting them that
they must be prepared to face. The great mystery of what's next is
represented by the east, and the teenage years are a time for exploration. We have a natural impulse to break away from family, as our
loyalty shifts from parents to peers. This is nature's way of getting us
out of the nest and launched. This can be both exciting and terrifying.
Teen years are confusing. It's not unusual to think our parents and
other adults are morons who don't know anything, while at the same
time still needing them and respecting them on a deeper level. Teens
reinvent the world generation after generation, and in so doing, they
face the same dangers that the great explorers have always faced. The
great unknown calls, and in answering that call, they don't know what
awaits or what they will encounter around the next bend.

Setting out on any adventure can be risky. Life does not offer any
guarantees, but in the big picture, making informed, heartfelt choices
yield the best results. That's why having a better understanding of who
we are and where we want to go in life can help as we make the very

serious decisions that are in front of us. It can give us something to measure a choice against rather than ideas given to us by others, even if they had our best interest at heart. Ultimately, like children ready to go off on their own, we have to make our own way in the world. But, at the same time, it is smart to ask for directions—or at least have a map in hand.

IMAGINATION:
A HEROIC COMPANION
ON THE ROAD

At no time in life is our imagination as unencumbered as it is during childhood. Reconnecting with our heart brings us untold opportunities to imagine life the way we want it. Albert Einstein once said, "Logic will get you from point A to point B, but imagination will take you everywhere." Our mind and all its calculations can take us only so far. Imagination lives in our heart where there is a world of limitless possibilities at our disposal. Yet we tend to think of imagination as make-believe and trivialize it. We forget that there's more to the process: *we create what we imagine.*

Imagination is one of the great, unsung heroes of healing and of living a vibrant life. It's how the medicine men do it. Noted Swiss psychiatrist Carl Jung introduced the concept of *active imagination* to the West in the early twentieth century, which, according to his memoir, he learned from an indigenous healer. It's a process of allowing the unconscious mind to express itself in images or story without interference from the narrative of the conscious mind (much like the practices offered in this book). It's a powerful process for shedding light on what's going on at deeper levels than rationalization.

Our authentic self is waiting in our heart. We can connect with this important aspect of ourselves through our imagination by picturing it and feeling it. From there, it becomes reality. It is our built-in ability to transcend whatever holds us back.

Further Explorations of the East

Choose one of the qualities associated with the east that resonates with you: innocence, hope, playfulness, curiosity, imagination, creativity, trust, openness, vulnerability, or joy. Write that quality in your journal. Spend time with it—in other words, just allow it to sit in your consciousness. You can go out for a walk or sleep on it. When you feel ready, find a comfortable place where you can be uninterrupted for 30 minutes or so. Close your eyes and place your hand over your heart. Take several deep breaths and imagine your life with this quality. Imagine yourself in a couple of typical experiences. How do you feel when this quality is available and you are expressing it? Where in your body does this quality resonate? Breathe into it. Bring life to it. Ask yourself what stands in the way of your fully embodying and experiencing this quality. Write your response in your journal, being as specific as possible. Ask yourself if you are ready to let this block be healed. Imagine what you will feel like when it is healed. Can you feel that now? You can repeat this process with other qualities, giving them time to take root in your heart or you can focus on the one you chose. Do what works best for you.

South:
Taking Down Walls
and
Mending Fences

Your task is not to seek love,
but merely to seek and find all the barriers
within yourself that you have
built against it.

~Rumi

Time of life:	Adult
Time of year:	Summer
Time of day:	Noon
Qualities:	Divine Feminine, courage, love, passion, relation-ship, procreation, will, generosity, endurance
Element:	Water
Spirit animal:	Coyote
Color:	Red
Embodiment:	Solar Plexus
Phrase:	Water, My Emotions

South symbolizes summer, and it corresponds to high noon. The sun is directly overhead warming the earth and ripening the garden. We feel Mother Earth's burning love in the power of the sun, and in the soft southern breeze, we find the gentleness of her caress. South is the place of warm rains and a soft green world. To our ancestors, summer was an easy time. Food and shelter were plentiful; life was good. South warms our hearts, bringing love to fruition. We know that for healthy love to flourish, it must be rooted in self-love.

On this journey around the wheel, south is where we explore our relationship to our emotions and our emotional patterns and tendencies that interfere with happy, balanced, passionate, loving relationships. Coyote is the spirit guide we call on, as Coyote is known for disrupting fixed patterns, and we are grateful for his help.

Water is the element of emotion. Water isn't fixed; it changes with the tides, with each bend in the river, and with a sudden rainstorm. Water reflects the changing nature of emotions. Someone once said relationships would be much easier if we didn't have any emotions involved. Someone else commented that without emotions there wouldn't be any relationships! Another double bind!

Water holds the imprint of consciousness of our epigenetic code as well as our own deep beliefs, emotions, hopes, and dreams. The late Masaru Emoto introduced the modern world to the living nature of water through his experiments on the effect of human consciousness on water. Since the human body is 50 to 65 percent water, as we move through life, the water in our bodies imprints with the energy of our thoughts, feelings, and actions.

A Matter of the Heart

The south gives us an opportunity to reflect on the recurring patterns of particular emotions we experience. We aren't our emotions; we are simply experiencing emotions. However, there is the matter of the chemistry of emotions to consider. When we experience various emotions, biochemicals flow through our bodies and affect all of our systems and organs, so in those moments, it's fair to say we are our emotions. Strong emotions interfere with our prefrontal cortex's ability to regulate our complex cognitive, emotional, and behavioral functioning. Once the tipping point has been reached, the chemicals need to be cleared from our body, which can take hours and even days. During this time, we are not completely present, and we need to take steps to become aware of our disconnection so that we can rein it in.

We can become addicted to the energy of emotions and the chemicals they create, just as we can become addicted to food or drugs. Adrenaline, for example, is appropriate for emergencies, but on a regular basis, it becomes a toxic cocktail that provides an emotional rush. It is often the force behind risky behavior, dangerous decisions, procrastination, overwork, chronic stress, and more. Self-inquiry goes on hold when we are in an anxiety pattern or when our emotions are all over the place or when we shut them off. All our relationships suffer, including our relationship with our self.

Likewise, while all emotions are part of the human condition, some have a greater tendency to cause problems than others. Anger, for example is a valuable tool, an alarm of sorts telling us we are not being treated fairly. It often indicates we aren't taking care of our own needs. Irregular mealtimes and unhealthy food choices can lead to a drop in blood sugar and a hair-trigger when it comes to anger. Sleep deprivation and overworking likewise contribute to anger. However, anger itself isn't the issue. We need to look deeper into what pattern has led us there. The same is true for the other emotions that are being expressed with negative results. Here are some questions to light the way:

- Do you experience cycles of anger, rage, sadness, fear, victimization?
- How do you express these emotions?
- Are these emotions relative to current situations or are they tied to stories and experiences from the past?
- Have your become attached to these stories and emotions?
- Are they helpful, or are they keeping you from living in the creative flow of today?
- Are you ready to release yourself from the patterns that are causing problems in your life?

South is the energy of the Divine Feminine. In the beauty and softness of south, we learn the power of gentleness in allowing ourselves to change. We gently shift our attachment to our emotions from our belly where they reside and place them in our heart where they can heal. Emotions aren't good or bad; they are part of the human experience. We don't need to try to control or repress them. They are the natural result of our experiences of life. It would be a flat horizon, indeed, without the highs and lows of a life lived with passion. (*Lust* is a synonym for passion, and generally speaking, our culture is intimidated by both!) Our Puritan ancestors sowed their seeds deeply.

We use the term *art* in talking about making these changes because healing, like art, wells up from within rather than as the result of a balm or a protocol applied from the outside. As we heal from the events in which our troubling emotions are rooted, their true value emerges, bringing heart-centered awareness. Emotions connect us to each other. They are the spice of life!

Taking responsibility for our emotions is a practice beginning with understanding that we can't change patterns when we are actively engaged in them. We need a glimmer of separation for the light of the south to penetrate. Our heart becomes the container into which we release our patterns. There's no judgment, no right or wrong—we simply take responsibility and shift our relationship from outside of us to within and make choices that reflect our true selves.

Loving Ourselves
Prepares Us for Loving Others

When we are talking about relationships that we hold in some level of endearment, the first relationship to look at is our relationship with ourselves. *How do I feel about me?* The commitment to love our inner child and to self-care that we made in the east began the process of developing self-love. Loving one's self, as Oscar Wilde wrote, "is the beginning of a lifelong romance." This romance shows up in our lives as lively enthusiasm for who we are, and it finds its way into everything we do. Loving another person is a reflection of how we love or don't love ourselves, so our primary relationship must always be with ourselves.

Not loving one's self creates a void inside that can take us down that familiar path we don't want to go. Not loving one's self neglects our most basic need to feel a sense of belonging, a loving connection that must be anchored in ourselves. We cannot fill each other's primal need for love, and we cannot expect others to do that for us. There is no escaping the reality that we must start with ourselves. If we don't love ourselves first, we have no love to share.

Family Patterns and Adult Relationships

The first step in changing a relationship pattern is awareness that, while it might be about "the other guy," it's also about us, and we're the only person we can actually change. That awareness may not seem earthshaking, but it is huge. Awareness of our patterns can be a great relief, but it can also bring sadness and anger. It takes time to process through the layers of emotions and feelings and sort through mistaken beliefs. In the south, the sun burns off the fog. Operating with a clear head is a much different experience than living by trial and error. As we unravel our family dynamics, we find the courage to create a healed vision of relationships. See "Got Some Unraveling to Do?" on pages 63–65.

GOT SOME UNRAVELING TO DO?

Effectively unraveling our family dynamics, learning from them, and moving past those inherited patterns might take a village, but we can start shedding light on our role in the family, on our memories and the feelings those memories evoke, as well as on our assumptions and impressions. This is a great start for pinpointing specific issues so that we can begin to resolve them, at least within ourselves.

On a large piece of heavy paper or poster board, write your name at the top. Write in the names of the members of your family in a row or rows on the bottom two-thirds of the paper, leaving space between them. The people you add might include extended family and people who aren't necessarily blood related but had a part in your life when you were growing up. (Write in small print so you can fit as much as you need to on the page.)

Draw a line connecting you to each of these people. Along that line, write in the overriding emotion you associate with that person, either yours or theirs. Jot down keywords that come up for you as you contemplate your relationship with that person. If specific memories with that person crop up, choose a word to represent that memory, circle it, and over that circle, write down the overriding emotion(s) associated with that memory. Under the person's name, list the qualities you associate with that person.

You can do this for each family member, one at a time, or switch back and forth between them. You can also draw additional lines attaching different family members to one another and jotting down your impression of their relationship and how you fit into it. If you like, you can also include events in the top one-third of the paper, using a key word to represent it, and attaching lines to all the people who were involved in those events, adding the overriding emotions along the connecting lines.

This is not an art project, and you don't even have to look at it again when you're finished. You also don't have to follow any rules. Once you get going, just allow what comes out of you to come. The more lines and words you have on the paper, the more unraveling you've done. What you're doing here is bringing your conscious awareness to all these thoughts and feelings twisted around one another in your subconscious mind. If this is particularly painful for you, share this activity with a trusted friend or counselor.

When you've completed your chart, ask yourself, "What is the story I have created about each of these people that's uniquely based on my experience with them?" Then ask, "Is that really who they are, or is that just my interpretation of them?"

Acknowledge that there is a lot more to each individual than you can ever know. None of us can know the whole story of anyone's life but our own. We don't know what their frame of reference was for why they did things the way they did them. If we're honest with ourselves, we realize that we don't even really completely understand our own frame of reference. And that's the point of our being here in this Heart Reconnection work: to better understand where we're operating from.

This process is a setup for forgiveness. If we're holding a grievance, a grudge, or a resentment toward someone in the family, we can come to realize that in the same way we're just doing the best we can do in the moment, each person in the family is also doing the best they can from where they're at and where they operate from. There is an opportunity here to begin to consciously let go. This might take a thousand tries, especially if it's an old resentment, before the energy clears, but keep at it.

General Stages of Romantic Relationships

Knowing that relationships naturally go through various stages can ease tension when we encounter uncertainties and struggles with those we are most intimate with. Family counselors describe anywhere from three to fifteen different stages that healthy relationships go through in the course of time. Here, we'll take a look at three general ones.

Stage One—Early Intimacy

Relationships begin with attraction and courtship. You meet, your heart beats faster, and the pursuit begins. You get a favorable response, and life couldn't be sweeter. The object of your affection is perfect in every way, and you feel the intensity of mutual attraction. As courtship moves into sexual relations, passions run high and are expressed through romance and lovemaking. Love chemicals enhance sex, bonding partners together. You literally cannot get to your prefrontal cortex, where the seat of reason lives, and you don't want to. Thus the expression "love is blind"! You are certain that you have found your soul mate. It all feels so right.

About a year or two into paradise, the intensity of the chemical rush wanes. Perhaps the body can't keep sustaining the high. Confusion bordering on panic ensues: *What's happening to us?* Reality without the love chemicals can get brutal. You blame each other or yourself. Arguments increase and become more destructive. Both of you feel tricked. *"You used to..."* becomes the new mantra. *"Well you didn't..."* is the response. Ideally, this is an invitation to go deeper into yourselves and come to terms with your personal history, family patterns, and the expectations for how you think it ought to be. But who knew? And if you did know, how would you have gone about "coming to terms"? The game has significantly changed, and this is a possible breakup time.

Stage Two—Power Struggles

The passion that was being expressed through romance and mind-blowing sex during the first part of the relationship is now being expressed through a power struggle. Anger, arguments, fights, and silent treatments threaten to take over. The relationship, if it survived the first stage, is in jeopardy again! This phase is natural and not unhealthy. It calls for new skills, particularly around communication and problem solving. If new skills aren't injected into the partnership at this point, your relationship will probably end, or you will fight for the rest of your lives. This assures passing these destructive patterns to your children. Divorce rates correspond to the rise and intensity of the power struggle.

Love has its irony. We might eventually find that the imperfect partner was the perfect person to push our buttons and push us into making changes. We may even discover that we were subconsciously attracted to each other in our effort to heal childhood wounds. But usually we don't understand what happened. This pattern stuff is hard to crack into and heal on your own. Patterns appear to be reality, an accurate description of life, not just your experience. When you've run into the same situation enough times, you begin to consider seeking advice. It really helps to have a flight plan and a pilot who has flown the route.

There's work to do alone and together to reap the benefits of partnership and to have a chance at the love you seek and deserve. The lessons can be intense, but like nature's interest in getting us mated, nature also wants us to wake up and be fully conscious. The wakeup call often comes in the form of heartbreak. Knowing more about the nature of a healthy relationship, rather than relying on the pop-culture version, and your willingness to take a hard look at yourself with someone to guide that process makes a big difference in how things turn out.

Stage Three—Safety and Security

On the other side of the struggle, there is calm water. You have developed healthy boundaries and learned how to manage conflict when it inevitably arises. You both realize that you can't change each other and have wisely given up trying. This is more like what you had in mind but didn't know you had to work so hard to get it. Couples who make it to this stage talk about falling in love all over again. They use words like *joy, satisfaction, peace,* and *playfulness.* Commitment deepens, and it's important to honor it. Some couples restate their vows or mark the change in some other significant way. Remember all the criticizing you did when things weren't going well? You might balance that with gratitude and celebration!

In many ways, this is just the beginning of your lives together, and ideally, this would be when marriage would occur. But most of us marry way before we know who we are and what goes into preparing for partnership. Most of the difficulties that came before this point were burning off family of origin karma. Regardless of our sincere desire to not repeat the past, we do unless we get to the roots and make creative changes.

SHEDDING MORE LIGHT ON INTIMATE RELATIONSHIPS

Being in an intimate committed relationship is a natural healthy part of adult life, but that doesn't mean we naturally know how to be successful at it. It isn't uncommon to get into an intimate partnership without being aware of who we are at our core or understanding how our family patterns influence how we operate on an interpersonal level. Some of us may avoid intimacy and commitment altogether because we're afraid of what might happen if we let someone get too close.

At this point in our journey, if we are in an intimate partnership that is suffering or has suffered because of something we've been doing, the south is the opportunity to start thawing out whatever is blocking us from truly connecting with our loved one. This isn't the time to make major decisions like divorce or separation. However, if we are at risk of injury—to body, mind, or sprit—due to a partner's behavior, that's the cue we need to seek advice from a professional to keep ourselves safe.

If we aren't presently in an intimate relationship at this point in our healing journey, it's a good idea to wait until we are fully in love with ourselves and we no longer feel blocked from sharing that love with others. This can take some time, and while we may feel lonely and desire that type of bond, we want to make sure that we are fully capable of giving another human being the love they deserve. Two good resources for embarking on a new relationship when that becomes the order of the day are the *Easy Does It Dating Guide* and the *Easy Does It Relationship Guide for People in Recovery,* both by by Mary Faulkner, MA.

Exploring the South

❧ Choose three symbols to represent relationships about which you are seeking insight, beginning with your relationship to yourself. The symbol can be something you find in nature, like a rock or shell or even a twig—or it can be something like a marble, a small trinket, etc. Spend a few minutes simply holding it in your hand and really connect with it. When you are ready, breathe into the symbol, and then hold it over your heart. Sit quietly and breathe deeply. On each exhalation, express gratitude for this opportunity. Feel how the symbol resonates in your body. In other words, feel the weight, the temperature, or any other physical sensations you experience. For example, you might observe "I am feeling heaviness," or "I'm feeling heat," or "I'm feeling jaggedness." The observation you make provides enough information; don't analyze it or try to create a reason for the sensation. After a few moments, move on to your next symbol and repeat the process. Afterward, journal about your experience and any insights you received. This kind of process goes to the roots and allows the subconscious to speak. That takes time. In the meantime, you are a question carrier, a noble position in the process of self-inquiry.

Disagreements Go with the Territory

Whether it is a platonic friendship or a romantic partnership, almost everyone who enters into a personal relationship with another human being expects that the relationship will bring happiness. Of course, this won't always be the case. Although fighting with someone we care about can be the result of a dysfunction, disagreements between people are completely natural. It is when conflict characterizes the relationship that it becomes a problem.

There are healthy ways to express our feelings, even strong ones, and ways to get our needs met without anyone getting hurt. Getting along doesn't mean compromising who we are; it means finding ways that allow both people in the relationship to be who they really are and express their personal truth. This is possible when we are free from the patterns of the past and have developed solid relationship skills. Heartfelt collaboration is one of those skills.

Heartfelt Collaboration versus Compromise

When it comes to problem solving, we tend to think of compromise, which is logical, and it should work. But it usually results in neither party getting their needs met. Heartfelt collaboration, on the other hand, finds solutions that leave both people satisfied. It works best if the partners in a relationship have identified values they share, which is a good idea itself. However, collaboration can work by identifying a mutual goal for the situation in question. Your goal can be as simple as: *We want something that we are both happy with*. Disagreement usually involves two people with conflicting ideas about how to make that happen!

The more the argument goes on, the more we dig in. Or one of the partners might withdraw, which stops the process. Both reactions yield poor results. Having a point of agreement to return to as the discussion gets more heated makes it possible to take a deep breath, go for a walk, or in some way let the chemistry settle down. We underestimate the chemistry factor. Once our emotions are aroused, it does not take long before they flood our system. It can take hours or days to process them out. In the meantime, even the slightest comment can trigger another full-scale blowout.

Heartfelt collaboration is generative, meaning it creates new possibilities beyond what either person expected. It takes us deeper into ourselves where something truly new can be found. It is an issue of trust. It requires laying aside solutions we are attached to and opening the space for working together in a creative process. Here's an example:

Rebecca is a morning person, and Jeff isn't. Rebecca had an important PowerPoint presentation to give at work on Monday and wanted to practice it on Jeff. It would take about an hour or so. Sunday wasn't an option because they had a family party to attend and would be spending a lot of time in the car. Rebecca wanted to do it on Saturday morning so she could go to the mall that afternoon to buy an outfit for the presentation. Jeff, however, looked forward to sleeping in. He told her he'd be available by noon, but that's when Rebecca was planning to head out for the mall. If one of them were to compromise, the other one would feel cheated, and this created tension. They thought about how they could both get their needs met; ultimately Jeff suggested they order dinner in on Saturday evening so that Rebecca could use the time she would normally spend cooking doing her presentation for Jeff. Rebecca agreed and picked up Jeff's favorite dessert on her way home from the mall. Both felt their needs had been met. It is in this way that heartfelt collaboration makes people happy and inspires cooperation.

It is wise to practice heartfelt collaboration in less tense situations before approaching a highly charged situation. Fortunately, or unfortunately (however you perceive it), we have myriad opportunities in our daily lives to practice this skill with those we love; it's often the little things that can be the most annoying, so that's a good place to start.

There are times when compromise is the quickest and most effective solution. In that case, it's important to take time to make sure each person is satisfied. We should be able to flip-flop the positions. If one person has to sacrifice more than the other, what consolation prize would swing the deal? For example, "If you help me in the yard this morning and skip the gym, I'll go for a bike ride with you afterward." This is a bit like score-keeping, but we do keep score, subconsciously. Trust is built on fairness. If one person is always or even mostly the one who submits to the other, there is a problem in the making. Ultimately, we find that collaboration produces the heartfelt solutions that build trust and create happiness.

Intentional Listening: The Five-Minute Miracle

"Are you listening to me? Did you even hear what I said?" How many times have you heard those questions or asked them of a partner, spouse, or friend. When asked, "How are you?" how often do you really tell the truth? When we are in the process of healing—and of everyday living—authentic communication is like a balm that allows a closed heart to open. Instead of making assumptions about how another person feels or projecting your story onto them, intentional listening brings you both into present time, *the only time that healing happens.*

The five-minute miracle of mindful communication allows time and space for both parties to bypass emotional reactivity and report their inner experience without judgment, anger, or annoyance. The ground rules include no blaming, shaming, or giving advice. This is a time for both people to speak from the heart and to be received with deep respect.

Both parties agree to allow each other to *talk without interruption* for five minutes. The job of the listener is not to talk back but to hear with their whole heart.

Here's how: Close your eyes and do a minute or two of deep breathing to relax. Then check in with your body and your feelings. For example, "I am feeling pretty stressed out. When I stop to notice, I feel super tense, particularly in my shoulders. I have so much work to do that I get panicky about how I will find time to do it. I feel myself actually tearing up, and then I stress myself out even more with negative thinking... and then—as you probably notice—I get cranky..."

When the first speaker finishes the five-minute monologue, the listener's job is to communicate empathy. "I heard you, and I'm sorry you feel so stressed" or whatever the appropriate response may be. Depending on the circumstance and the person, this may be the moment for a hug, but it's not a time to give advice. Instead, both parties close their eyes, breathe to relax, and then the listener has a turn to speak and be acknowledged.

It's fine if you run out of things to say. Just sit together in the silence. When both parties have spoken and have been graciously received, you can continue your respectful listening in conversation. Most people who do this exercise are astonished at how good it feels to actually be listened to. It reduces stress, boosts intimacy, and creates that precious feeling of well-being we all crave.

HEART-CENTERED RELATIONSHIP TOOLBOX

1. **Practice non-defensiveness.** If you start to bristle when you are corrected, take a deep breath and open your mind and heart. Listen and respond with curiosity and patience.

2. **Practice peace.** The ability to calm yourself down—what's called self-regulation—is essential to relating from your heart rather than reacting from past conditioning.

3. **Your time is the most important gift you have to give.** Set aside dedicated time to be with friends and loved ones. Turn off the TV, power off your devices, and be present for each other.

4. **Give time to yourself.** Recharging your batteries by taking time to do something you enjoy every day lifts your mood and reduces burnout and stress. Remember that your most important relationship is with yourself.

5. **Inquire about others.** While it's fine to talk about yourself, don't hog all the airtime. There is more than one person in the universe, and everyone deserves to be heard.

6. **Think *we* instead of *me*.** Important decisions that you make for yourself are likely to affect those close to you as well. So be sure to negotiate, including them in your deliberations.

7. **Express your needs clearly.** Other people can't read your mind, and if you think they should, resentment is sure to build up.

8. **Say please and thank you.** We learn to do this as kids, and it's still necessary as adults. Being gracious to others usually results in their being gracious to you. Everyone thrives on respect, gratitude, and recognition.

9. **Be willing to say you're sorry.** When you make a mistake, get grouchy, or space out on a responsibility, be prompt to admit it and apologize sincerely.

10. **Give honest compliments.** Recognizing good things about other people and sharing them is a kindness that can make someone's day.

Gordon's Relationship Styles:
Soul to Soul versus Role to Role

As with all things in life, when it comes to our relationships, we inherit the frames of reality of our family and communities. South asks, "Are these frames, filters, beliefs, and ways of living in the world absolute truths? Are they cast in stone?" Author Parker Palmer reminds us of the importance of maintaining our connection with our inner life and our outer life (*The Voice of Vocation*).

We bring expectations into our relationships, and there are times when there is a mismatch form the start. One person is looking for one thing, and the other is looking for something else. We can look at relationship as role to role, such as work relationships or a deeper soul to soul. Neither type of relationship is right or wrong; the question is about appropriateness and expectation. It can be very challenging to try to find soul-to-soul fulfillment from a role-to-role relationship—and equally challenging to try to compress a soul-to-soul relationship into a role.

A role-to-role relationship might be a professional one where we do something for someone in exchange for pay. The issue arises when we expect our job to be fulfilling on a heart-and-soul level. The reverse can also occur: we might take a job expecting it to be about nothing more than paying the bills and find ourselves intrigued and inspired. Life is like that; we don't really know what anything is for sure until we are in it. We can talk about the water being cold, but it's not real until we jump in. Personal relationships work the same way.

ASSESSING OUR RELATIONSHIPS ROLES

Divide a piece of paper in half and label one half "Role to Role" and the other "Soul to Soul." Think about what these terms represent to you and which of your relationships might fall within each category. What roles do you play in life? Son/daughter, mother/father, sister/brother, husband/wife, girl-friend/boyfriend, student/teacher, boss/worker, giver/receiver, performer/onlooker, etc. Do these roles represent your personal truth, or are they just roles you play? Have you confused any of these roles with who you are at your core? Now, think about which of your relationships fall under the soul-to-soul category. What characterizes such relationships? Some ideas include honesty, vulnerability, clarity, expression, and mutual respect. How does a soul-to-soul relationship feel compared to a role to role? What is rewarding about one or the other?

Again, this is not about judging, as both types of relationships have a place in our human experience. This exercise is about finding clarity on what we are doing and where we are living from in our relationships, regardless of whether that relationship is personal, professional, familial, or social. This exercise opens us up to owning the deeper truth of the choices we are making and the relationships we are fostering.

Further Explorations of the South

ತಿ Choose one of the qualities associated with the south that
resonates with you: Divine Feminine, courage, love, passion, relationship, procreation, will, generosity, endurance.
Write that quality in your journal. Spend time with it — in other
words, just allow it to sit in your consciousness. You can go
out for a walk or sleep on it. When you feel ready, find a comfortable place where you can be uninterrupted for 30 minutes
or so. Close your eyes and place your hand over your heart.
Take several deep breaths and imagine your life with this
quality. Imagine yourself in a couple of typical experiences.
How do you feel when this quality is available and you are
expressing it? Where in your body does this quality resonate?
Breathe into it. Bring life to it. Ask yourself what stands in the
way of your fully embodying and experiencing this quality.
Write your response in your journal, being as specific as possible. Ask yourself if you are ready to let this block be healed.
Imagine what you will feel like when it is healed. Can you feel
that now? You can repeat this process with other qualities,
giving them time to take root in your heart or you can focus on
the one you chose. Do what works best for you.

West:
Investigating the
Shadow

Re: Shadow:
Often, it's not about becoming a new person,
but becoming the person you were meant to be,
and already are, but don't know how to be.

~Heath L. Buckmaster,
American author

Time of life: Mature Adult/Early Elder

Time of year: Fall

Time of day: Sundown

Qualities: Wisdom and acceptance, deep insight, self-understanding, wholeness, healing

Element: Air

Spirit animal: Bear

Color: Black

Embodiment: Brow

Phrase: Air, My Mind

West represents the fall of the year and the approaching sundown. Shadows grow long as the sun descends in the west. This is a time in the cycle when the seeds of lessons learned sprout wisdom. With maturity comes the awareness that the wisdom is there, beyond the shadows. Our question that has propelled this journey is *Who am I?* This question cannot be answered without speaking with the shadow.

West is the direction of air and is located in our mind. In our culture, mind is considered our finest quality, upheld over heart and soul. However, mind is subject to conditioning, and once it accepts an idea, it tends to hold on to it. Unless we intentionally work toward balancing our heart and our mind, our thinking is distorted. Natural commonsense solutions don't engage the mind; it prefers complication over simplicity. Without connection and balance with heart, we can't think clearly. Our thoughts get stale; we become inflexible, jaded, fearful, and defensive. Qualities such as compassion, empathy, and imagination are centered in our heart and soul. Mind is not the enemy; however, it must be balanced with the heart.

In our reflections on the wheel, we learn to sit with our mind and make peace with mind and heart. We practice the realization that we are *not* our mind or heart. We are the one who hears our thoughts and feels our feelings. We are the witness to these aspects of our being human. This is at the heart of the Buddhist practices.

We learn how to avoid judging our thoughts, knowing that we can't judge our mind into submission; it draws energy from the argument. Nor can we beat the mind into submission. The element of west is air, and just as we can't beat the wind into submission, we can't beat the mind into submission. Key to rebalancing this relationship is to understand and acknowledge the mind's strengths and its weaknesses, and not expect it to do what it can't do—feel the pain of others. To reclaim balance with our mind, we come to our mind as an adult comes to a wounded child, with calm nonjudgmental love and patience. This is a profound practice in our life, and it shifts the angst and conflict surrounding the need to be right or the reactions from self-judgment and fear. Without the balance of the mind, our feelings, emotions, empathy, and compassion can overwhelm us. Like everything else, balance is the answer.

Once we learn to listen to the mind without reaction and gently shift our attention to the heart, we can relieve our mind of having to be responsible for us. Our mind was designed to help with life; it was not intended to be the boss. Likewise, our emotions and feelings are part of a system that, when put in proper relations, brings wholeness.

The Theory of the Shadow

West draws us within to meet an aspect of ourselves that we have kept hidden. Meeting and accepting our shadow brings wisdom and wholeness. Yet, looking into our dark side requires courage. We are here to heal.

Swiss psychiatrist Carl Jung, whose work was as spiritually oriented as it was psychological, developed the theory of shadow to identify aspects of our psyche that, for many reasons we have ignored or intentionally hidden. In *Psychology and Religion* (1938), Jung wrote, "Everyone carries a shadow, and the less it is embodied in the individual's conscious life, the blacker and denser it is.... If it is repressed and isolated from consciousness, it never gets corrected." We need to meet our shadow and allow it into the light to heal and to experience our wholeness. We can finally let go of trying to be perfect; we can quit hiding our "flaws." We can move on with our life's journey feeling good about ourselves.

THE VOICE OF THE SHADOW

You, yes, you over there in the sunshine. You grab at the light, and you curse the darkness. But I hold the key to your wholeness. It only comes by accepting all of you: the good, the bad, the beautiful, and the not-so-pretty aspects. That's where I come in. As your infamous Shadow, I have a story to tell, and if you dare to listen, I can help us both grow in wisdom and compassion. There is no light without darkness, no up without down, no hot without cold, no hope without despair. What do you say? Are you ready to meet me?

Why Investigate the Shadow?

When we first hear about the shadow, we automatically think it's bad. But our shadow often has the key to important parts of us. It can be the child discouraged by an early failure that holds us back from expressing our truth. Our shadow might have the key to unlocking our creativity. It might sit down at the computer and write a best seller. Or it might be an adventurous part of us that wanted to forego college to sail around the world. In short, it is probably much more innocent and interesting than we would ever suspect.

We are shaped by the time and place we inhabit. We didn't always meet the standards set for us, but we knew how to get the love we needed, conditional as it was. We hid the parts that didn't meet expectations. We banished, suppressed, repressed, and exiled them to the underworld of the subconscious.

In truth, characteristics of the shadow are made of the natural human quirks and qualities that we've been told are unacceptable. Who is "in" and who is "out" are influenced by our family, friends, school, religion, and the culture at large—most likely, a combination of these factors. In polite society, we call conditioning socialization, training, education, being taught good manners, and so on. Whatever the influences were, we made ourselves smaller to fit into the narrow boxes prescribed for us by others. Or we took way too much on for the same reason: to fit in.

When we reach a certain stage in our lives and realize that we no longer want to sacrifice what is most unique to us, we become more curious about our shadow, and our sincere investigation begins. Investigation can result in incredible opportunities we hadn't thought were possible before. This is our stepping into possibilities, new choices, options, and a new relationship to life. As we learn the backstory of our beliefs and choices, we learn that we can undo the agreements and beliefs that do not fit our reality. That is something the shadow is particularly good at.

Honesty and willingness to step up bring clarity as our awareness expands. This is not an easy walk, but it is a huge gift to us and to our relations. The challenges that come up offer the opportunity to demonstrate belief in ourselves by showing up and taking the next step, even when our personality may not want to. We can turn back, give up, and settle for where we are, or we can reach down into our depths and pull up our tenacity, patience, and staying power and bring them into the light. We can question and sit and wait for answers and new understandings. We can free ourselves from old judgments, beliefs, and patterns. As we step into the light, we step into the unknown, and we find the grace of truth within.

A BRIGHTER LIGHT

When we keep our fear and shame in the darkness, they block our creativity and disconnect us from our instincts and from our heart. They get us second-guessing ourselves: We hold back when we should go for it and go for it when we should hold back. When we accept our whole self, our light shines brighter and good things find us. Here are two examples:

When Ryan met his shadow, he walked away from a six-figure salary at an advertising agency to become a schoolteacher. As a kid, he had dreams of being a teacher, but his dad had told him that *those who can, do, and those who can't, teach.* Though Ryan didn't exactly understand what that saying meant, the sarcasm in his father's voice spoke volumes, so Ryan shoved his calling into the shadow. Ryan was so good at teaching that he became kind of a legend in his hometown. Eventually, he ran for mayor and won. Of course, the new mayor is in favor of increasing the school's budget.

Diana's shadow showed her a character that she calls her Inner Bitch. Though she works in a highly competitive profession, she often held herself back because she didn't want to make waves. She'd grown up believing she had to be "nice" to make her way in the world. However, meeting her Inner Bitch was just what she needed to kick a hole in the glass ceiling. She got the promotion she deserved, and now she lets her Inner Bitch out whenever she feels it's necessary.

Meeting Our Shadow

To get an idea of what our shadow might look like, we can observe the people around us. Qualities that we are drawn to in other people, as well those that we are repelled by, give us clues about what we've kept hidden inside ourselves. Chances are, whatever we admire as well as what we judge harshly live within us.

Exploring the West

ः Think of five people in your life, and make a list in your journal of the qualities you like about them or qualities you don't like about them, or both. Keep in mind that this isn't about those particular people. It is something within you awakening. Your awareness to these qualities in others sheds light on your shadow.

℃ In your journal, list three qualities you admire about yourself
in one column. Then, in a second column, identify what you
think are the opposites of those admirable qualities. During
this process, your shadow will begin to emerge. There's noth‐
ing you need to know or do other than sit with your discoveries
and let the shadow tell you its story.

Getting to Know Our "Inner Community"

Many of us are familiar with our inner committee, those discor‐
dant voices in our head, nagging and berating us for virtually every‐
thing we say and do or don't say and do. What we may not be as
familiar with are the helpful aspects of ourselves, the archetypal quali‐
ties that live in us as our "inner community." Jung used the concept
of the archetype to identify universal characteristics that reside in the
collective unconscious of the human psyche.

Archetypes are resources. Their skills or qualities add dimension
to our personalities, taking us beyond ourselves to connect with our
potential. Similar to the shadow, archetypes are awakened within
us when we encounter their qualities in other people. We might be
attracted to a certain person or a character in a play, film, poem, or
novel. Our attraction to those characteristics resonates with similar
characteristics in our psyche that want to be expressed, and that arche‐
type becomes an active member of our inner world, and it's on our side.

Incorporating our archetypes into our conscious mind can get us
past our programming and conditioning. It already exists in us. The
invitation is to allow ourselves to fully engage the archetype, experi‐
encing and expressing it. The following table offers insight into some
of the various archetypes and their qualities.

Using this table, we can begin to identify those we embody, those we can imagine activating in the future, and those that don't hold any attraction for us.

ARCHETYPE	QUALITIES
ARTIST	Imaginative, sees potential, sensitive, seeks change, a transformer (all forms of creativity)
CHILD	Innocent, vulnerable, playful, hopeful, forgiving, open, naïve, positive outlook
FOOL	Unconventional, in the moment, innovative, finds a way around any situation, transformer, lives by their own rules
JUDGE	Fairness, thoughtful, neutral, decision maker
KING OR QUEEN	Takes charge, self-control, leads others, dignified, makes decisions by proclamation
LOVER	Embraces diversity, charming, charismatic, enchanting, sensuous, finds beauty everywhere, heart, transformer
PARENT	Nurtures and protects, loves and offers unqualified acceptance
SAGE/WISE ONE	Offers balanced perspective, nonjudgmental, sees the big picture, understands the human journey and has experienced much of it
SEEKER	Explores inner and external world, willing to give up security for community, intimacy for autonomy, spontaneous
SHAMAN (PRIEST, RABBI, ETC.)	Grounded in principles and ethics, open minded and open hearted, carries our highest ideals, transformer

| SKEPTIC | Cautious, wants a free trial on everything, researches facts and figures before committing |
| WARRIOR | Defender, rescuer, brave, disciplined, lives by a strict code, will fight to the end |

Each archetype has a negative expression, along with its helpful side. The negative expression of the Parent archetype might be *"smothers, controlling, or abandons."* This gives a more complete and understanding of the archetype and of ourselves. The qualities we have identified are used as examples. As you add your insight, the exercise broadens and becomes a more powerful teacher. Exploring archetypes certainly adds dimension to the question, *Who am I?*

Further Explorations of the West

- ☙ Spend time with each archetype listed in the table on pages 87–88. Connect with the experience of being this aspect or imagining being this aspect. Give the character a name. Come up with some examples of when you have acted out of this character both positively and negatively. See if that character feels included and appreciated. Are there other archetypes you wish you had? The following questions help you get a sense of this archetype: *How does this character dress? What kind of music does it prefer? Food? Activities? Movies? Where does this character go on Saturday night? What would this character's motto be?*

- ☙ Choose one of the qualities associated with the west that resonates with you: wisdom and acceptance, deep insight, self-understanding, return to wholeness, healing. Write that quality in your journal. Spend time with it—in other words, just allow it to sit in your consciousness. You can go out for a walk or sleep on it. When you feel ready, find a comfortable place where you can be uninterrupted for 30 minutes or so. Close your eyes and place your hand over your heart. Take several deep breaths and imagine your life with this quality. Imagine yourself in a couple of typical experiences. How do you feel when this quality is available and you are expressing it? Where in your body does this quality resonate? Breathe into it. Bring life to it. Ask yourself what stands in the way of your fully embodying and experiencing this quality. Write your response in your journal, being as specific as pos-sible. Ask yourself if you are ready to let this block be healed. Imagine what you will feel like when it is healed. Can you feel that now? You can repeat this process with other qualities, giving them time to take root in your heart or you can focus on the one you chose. Do what works best for you.

 C8 Try the "Centering Practice" below. The directions are simple, so there's no need to narrate a script.

CENTERING PRACTICE: BALANCE BETWEEN HEART WISDOM AND MIND REASON

Sit in a comfortable position with your feet on the floor, hands in your lap, and your back straight so that you can hold energy through your spine.

Breathe deeply and slowly, connecting to the frequency of light that is your presence in your body. Use your imagination to see yourself as the light or energy that gives life to your physical body.

Bring your awareness to your heartbeat. As you focus on your heartbeat, give your heart a voice, and say from your heart to your mind, *Peace be with you.* Feel the energy of the offering of peace from your heart to your mind. Imagine your mind accepting the energy of peace—relaxing and breathing.

Next, turn it around. Your mind offers to your heart, *And peace be with you.* Direct that energy from your mind to your heart. Imagine your heart accepting the energy of peace—relaxing and breathing.

Sit for five minutes in this exchange between heart and mind, of peace and balance, breathing in and out, letting go of any distractions. When you are done, go in peace.

⁂

There is no good reason for us to live in conflict between heart wisdom and mind reason; both are simply aspects of being human. And when we, as the adult in relation to all our human aspects, step into the center of our life and being, we take the lead as the one responsible for each choice we make. Of course, we still have fears and anxiety, but we learn to separate our true self from our stories, roles, and labels. We hold sacred space for ourselves, allowing us to choose how we will live our life from moment to moment.

CHAPTER
9

North: Discovering Mystery, Wisdom, and Dreamtime

In our deepest moments of struggle, frustration,
fear, and confusion, we are being called upon to reach in and
touch our hearts. Then, we will know what to do, what to say,
how to be. What is right is always in our deepest heart of
hearts. It is from the deepest part of our hearts that we are
capable of reaching out and touching another human being.
It is, after all, one heart touching another.

~Roberta Sage Hamilton

Time of life: Elder, Sage, Teacher, and Healer

Time of year: Winter

Time of day: Midnight

Qualities: Transformer, wisdom keeper, spinner of dreams, contemplative, accepting, nurturing, humble, visionary

Element: Fire

Spirit animal: Turtle

Color: White

Embodiment: Crown (just above the top of the head)

Phrase: Fire, My Spirit

North offers solitude and quietness for reflection, gifts our spirit guide Turtle brings. Turtle moves slowly and close to the ground. The long dark nights lend themselves to dreaming. Just as we traditionally retreat into the warmth of our homes in the winter, north calls us inside, into ourselves. We connect with the Great Mystery and with our ancestors, our loved ones, and our place on the earth.

North settles us into our body, bringing insight into how we will choose to live our life from here forward. *The wisdom we have acquired is in our bones*; it is the new structure supporting our thoughts, our feelings, and our experiences; it has the power to bring direction and purpose to our life.

Deciding where you want to go or what you want to explore and taking that into action is what life is all about. Heading out on your own without the basic life skills, however, is foolhardy. Prior investigation, preparation, and an idea of the skills you need make sense.

Talk with people and listen to their experiences of what you want to do. You'll be surprised at how lively the conversation becomes and how much you learn. Everyone likes to swap stories and share adventures. Listening is a wise practice of good relations.

Reflecting on the Journey Thus Far

Sitting with the fire, we reflect on the journey around the wheel. Whether it is our first or fifteenth time, we are awakening to deeper and deeper aspects of our true heart and spirit. You have sought self-understanding through the question, *Who am I?*

Take time to sit with that question and write your discoveries in your journal. You won't have the complete picture yet, but what have you discovered? You can write a letter to yourself telling yourself what you've learned. This approach provides a different perspective. The following are suggestions to get you started:

- You traveled into the east, into the dawn of your new life and met your newborn self. *What have you learned through revisiting childhood patterns?*
- You stood in the south in the heat of the sun and explored hidden patterns and epigenetic inheritance to prepare for healthy, loving relationships. *You are here now, living your life; what do you choose to give belief to?*
- You faced the end of the day in the west as the sun slipped into the sea, and you delved deep into your subconscious to meet your shadow. *What did you discover?*
- You have asked the question, *Who am I?* How do you answer that question now?

Claiming Your Fire Spirit

Moving around the wheel, we have been healing, releasing, shifting, awakening, and opening. We have greater awareness of ourselves and who we really are beneath all the old stories and roles we were once attached to. Fire Spirit is a transformer. It changes matter into energy, light, smoke, ash, and heat. It is a shape-shifter, always moving, changing, and shifting its place and its form. You are the Fire Spirit consciousness that animates your body and gives it life.

When we leave the body, it will return to the earth, and our spirit will return to the realms of the spirit world. We are being born into the Fire Spirit! We are transforming our relations to ourselves first, and the rest of life second. We have taken full responsibility for our lives and choices. We honor our heart-centered awareness by respecting what was written on our heart by our creator. We are whole and beautiful. We will live in respectful relations with ourselves and with all others. We have gratitude and humility in this great opportunity to be who we are.

By our Fire Spirit, we find resilience and strength to keep stepping into our next moment. The question *Who am I?* is not so scary anymore because we have found that spark of truth within us. Just as the White Buffalo Calf Woman reminds the Lakota people of what is truly sacred in life, we too are reminded that we are sacred, all our relations are sacred, and life is sacred.

Practice makes the master, and we have many tools for our continued awakening to our healing path to freedom. Here in the north, we relax by the fire. Slowing down invites wisdom to come forward. Our heart is beating now, and it is up to us to breathe with that heartbeat, honor our truth, and exercise our courage to live the path of authenticity.

In the north, we have the opportunity to practice true forgiveness, letting go of the old energies we clung to because we did not know any better. The gift of forgiveness allows us to be energetically free from attachments to old traumas, heartbreaks, and fears that have haunted us. We didn't understand that the threads of our judgment kept us attached to those stories and experiences.

Once we let go and gave it to the fire, the energy of suffering and fear was transformed and recycled throughout the cosmos. This practice of forgiveness frees us as the wheel moves us toward a new spring in the east. The journey of the seasons and the medicine wheel continues throughout life, season by season, day by day, choice by choice, with gratitude and love for our true self, our relations, our friends, and the Great Mystery.

THE POWER OF CONSCIOUS AWARENESS

As we journey around the medicine wheel, we come to the power of conscious awareness. Our understanding of life and what it means to be alive, seasoned with time, deepens and broadens. Awareness of death draws closer, and we contemplate regeneration through dreaming a dream for fellow travelers and those who have just begun their journey. We are grateful for the power of our dreams. We can appreciate lessons learned and claim our wisdom.

Coming Together

North is the coming together time; it is when we gather around the fire with our community. We have done deep soul-searching, and we now can relax and be easy in reflecting on our journey. This is a community of respect, diversity, creativity, and maturity. We heal in community, find support in community, and create in community, all the while reclaiming belief in ourselves. True healthy community reflects the uniqueness of its members. Free of the old fears that drove us to want to be like others as security, we have found faith in our personal truth and respect for ourselves, which translates to respect for others' unique expression of their lives. As we come to fully accept ourselves, we naturally accept others. We get what we give.

Through our journey of healing and self-discovery, our passion for dreams is kindled and comes to life. Possibilities are our new allies, and by the practices of patience and self-reliance, we have the intent to follow through in manifesting our dreams.

Exploring the North

ᘓ The long dark winter provides much time for dreaming. Think about your answers to the following questions and express those answers silently, in art, in words, and/or aloud to others—or to your reflection.

- What do you dream for yourself? See it now. Draw it. Write it. Speak it.

- What do you dream for Mother Earth and the life upon her? See it now. Draw it. Write it. Speak it.

- Who are your friends and family? Who is part of your community? See it now. Draw it. Write it. Speak it.

CS Write a short story about your real, true, authentic, responsible, here's-who-I-am, here's-what-I-want kind of life. What does this type of life look like to you? This isn't about writing a perfect essay, but if you don't feel comfortable writing, record yourself telling the story. You can even make a collage using pictures and words if you prefer.

Wisdom Practices for a Strong, Joyful Spirit, No Matter the Season

With the north comes a perfect time for inner reflection, which strengthens our spirit and keeps our heart fire burning even in the coldest of winters. However, we don't need to retreat under the covers. We can create a rich environment in our lives that reflects our inner world into our outer world, giving us even more opportunity to reflect on the life we are leading and where we are headed. The following are seven practices to help us clear a path. Though they are listed in a linear fashion, no one practice is more important than another, like spokes on a wheel.

Recharge

Winter symbolizes our ongoing need for downtime regardless of the time of year. We need time to rest and appreciate life. We need to sleep well at night and rest throughout the day even if it's only a few minutes. We need time to feel the feelings that go with our experiences; that's how we learn. We have a tendency to push through life as if it is a race. Wisdom is knowledge gained through experience. It takes time to mulch experiences into lessons learned. Transformation happens when our brains slow down.

Downtime is a period of inactivity—not sleep necessarily, but rest. It's cool spiritual medicine. Our central nervous system, which pretty much runs our show, has two basic cycles: rest and action. Healing goes on during the rest cycle. It's like charging our phone battery when it gets low. If we don't plug it in, we're going to get disconnected. Without adequate restoration, even normal everyday stress will deplete our energy; we basically run out of battery life. What might happen when we're operating on a low or depleted battery? There's a long list of possibilities: bad moods, poor decisions, aches and pains, indigestion, low/high blood pressure, reduced susceptibility to illness, and so on.

In the east, we made a commitment to get enough sleep. Now, we are making a commitment to just let our bodies have a break from all the usual physical and mental activities it needs to engage in as part of living. The medicine wheel is all about healing the body, mind, and spirit; it's about cultivating coolness. When we balance action with rest, our bodies are in a better, stronger position to handle whatever's going around—whether it's physical, mental, spiritual, or emotional.

The following winter activities, while active, can still be considered downtime:

- Take a yoga class.
- Go cross-country skiing.
- Walk in the falling snow.
- Make snow angels.

- Make your own calendar. Use pictures you like or draw your own and mark the important dates. Keep it where it's handy and make notes on it before going to bed.
- Find a good book at the library and read it. You can get audio books if reading isn't your thing. Explore a topic that interests you.
- Visit an art museum.
- Look up soup recipes and try them out. Maybe invite a friend or two to join you for a bowl of soup and a movie.

Commune with Nature

Mother Nature is powerful spirit medicine. We sometimes think of nature as something we walk around on or look through the window at. We forget or ignore that our bodies are made up of the same minerals and elements as the ground we walk on, as the tree we see through the window, as the bird that flies past our line of vision. We are *nature*. Earth is an element of the north, and it calls us to spend time with our kin by venturing out of our concrete shells to touch the grass with our toes, brush our palm against a tree trunk, dip our fingertips in a cool stream, gaze up at the trees towering above our heads. We need to spend at least a little time in and with nature as often as possible. This can be as simple as opening a window to breathe in the fresh air and admire the scenery if we can't venture fully outside or as involved as hiking a mountain to its peak. Spending downtime with our animal companions can also bring us closer to the earth.

Be Open

Healing is about cleaning house inside and outside. This cannot be accomplished if the doors are shut or our way through is too cluttered.

An open mind and open heart are strong medicine. Being open allows room for honest assessment with the very real possibility for transformation. As we step into this new time in our lives, what do we want to bring with us? We have the choice to take on new beliefs, see new possibilities, and even develop a new attitude. We can also change our mind about things if we choose to. We are always in process, and new awareness is always coming to us. We just need to trust our sense of things and trust life. We can make growing a positive attitude part of our spiritual practice. When we set our intention on living a life that has meaning for us, we open ourselves up to possibilities.

Play

Fun is joyful medicine. Amusement and enjoyment are health-promoting celebrations of life. Knowing how to play should be easy, but oftentimes, life has been such that we've forgotten how to kick back and laugh. When we're consciously making time for play, there will usually be a learning curve before we can fully get back into the groove. We can start with something small like coloring. These days, adult coloring books are all the rage, but for a good reason: coloring is fun. Kids know it, and at some point, we knew it too. We can also hang out with people who know how to have good clean fun and learn from their lead. As author Roald Dahl once said, "A little nonsense now and then is relished by the wisest men."

Practice Gratitude

Appreciation is sweet to the spirit. To express our gratitude, we practice thinking "thank-you" thoughts in place of "WTF?" thoughts. For example, is the glass half full or half empty? It doesn't matter; it's just *Thank you for the glass and the beverage it contains.* In this way, our awareness shifts from what we don't have to what we do have. When we redirect our attention to what we are grateful for, our body chemistry changes immediately. It boosts our immune system, normalizes blood pressure, and makes an uncountable number of other healthy adjustments in mind, body, and spirit. It creates positive energy inside of us and around us. Positive energy is attractive. Making a conscious decision to interrupt negativity and nurture a loving attitude makes our heart happy, which is a powerful defense against slipping back into a dark hole.

> Be grateful for luck, don't mind the thunder,
> listen to the birds and don't hate nobody.
>
> ~Eubie Blake (1887–1983),
> Composer and Ragtime pianist

Reimagine

Our heart is curious; it wants to explore all possibilities and grows stronger when we give our imagination free reign. Imagination is magical spiritual medicine. It helps us to see that all things are possible. We may have become adept at imagining our lives in a less than desirable light, but if we're good at that, we can be equally as good at, if not better at, reimagining ourselves having all the qualities we desire. We can also use our imagination to experience what it would feel like if we magically accepted parts of ourselves that we've had trouble accepting. Pretend, and act *as if*. That's what imagination is good for. We create what we imagine. What nice thing would we like to see happen for Mother Earth and all her creatures? Let's imagine it now.

Breathe!

Our breath is the quintessential spiritual medicine. Without a regular dose of it we... well, we wouldn't be able to read any further! Inspiration is the intake of spirit; it is our spiritual connection. When in doubt, breathe. When anxious, breathe. When scared, breathe. When tempted, breathe. Taking six deep breaths, filling our bellies and expanding our lungs with the life-giving air surrounding us, can improve conditions in our internal world, no matter what's going on "out there." Six more make it mo' better. We need to keep breathing to remain inspired.

GETTING SLEEPY?

In his book *The Twenty Minute Break*, Ernest L. Rossi, PhD, describes the body's naturally occurring process call the ultradian rhythm. Every 90 minutes or so, it automatically switches from the sympathetic nervous system (the active side) to the parasympathetic nervous system (the restful side), during which time all of our systems are refreshed, including body, mind, and spirit. If something needs healing, this is when it is addressed. It takes anywhere from 10 to 30 minutes and then naturally switches back to the active cycle. During that brief time, the body monitors and refreshes the organs. The events of the preceding couple of hours have been sorted and filed.

This restful side is usually the time when we start feeling spaced out. Yawning is a signal that we are switching to the parasympathetic side. It gets hard to focus. Most of the time, we respond by taking a trip to the vending machine or coffee pot, telling ourselves to wake up because there's work to be done! However, if you have the chance to lie down or place your head back against the chair for 10 minutes, you can take advantage of this stress-reducing natural rhythm rather than try to fight it.

See if you can notice your ultradian rhythm throughout the day and enjoy it when you can. Notice any changes in your health, emotional life, and general well-being, and record your discoveries in your journal.

Releasing the Energy of "I Am Less Than"

North gives us insight into the legacy we carry in our blood. Through the malleable nature of our genes, we are imprinted with the energetic experiences of our ancestors. We literally carry their legacy in our blood and DNA. The beauty of our willingness to heal and our tenacity of spirit is that we are not just healing from our lifetime; we are healing that legacy that runs back through the generations. Our healing is a gift both to those who came before us and to the generations yet to come.

We can clear our field by releasing our *attachment* to our feelings of failure, of not being enough, or any of the brokenness we carry and the stories we keep repeating and allow it all to be transformed into something that reflects our best self. Whether it is a behavior, belief, identity, or story—whatever it was that held the energy of brokenness must be let go. Here we say:

My name is _____,
*and I am a human being. Yes, I have been brokenhearted,
anxious, fearful, compulsive, out of balance, and out of
control, and none of those words are who I am. They were
energies, roles, dependencies, addictions, and other aspects
of human life that I created over time through repetition,
belief, indulgence, and/or reaction, but those aspects of my
life's experience do not define me. My personal truth is who I
am. I release my attachments to all beliefs that do not reflect
the truth of my soul.*

From the place of the north, we have the opportunity to sit with
all this and notice how these concepts feel in our body. It is through
reconnecting to our intuitive wisdom that we can become clear on
what feels correct and what does not. As human beings, we are 100
percent responsible for what we choose to believe, and through our
Heart Reconnection journey, we are reclaiming our ability to shift
our awareness from living solely by the mind's voices to listening and
feeling the body's deeper wisdom.

The body never lies; the conditioned mind is fearful and more
determined to be "right" than to acknowledge the truth. When threat-
ened, the mind spins our broken story, our wounded tale. That sets
off a chain reaction in the body that leads to physically *feeling* bad
and confused. The body has a more grounded sense of what it knows.
It doesn't have the need to be "right." Our body wants to live and
be healthy and would probably love to be rid of the mind's conditioning. Both mind and body are aspects of being human and make
their unique contributions to living life in this world. It is, as always,
a matter of balance. Mind tends to take over the system because it

is prized by our culture; it has been reinforced for centuries as the quality that gives us superiority over all the creatures. Apparently it hasn't spent much real time with a hungry tiger. Our heart has the key to finding the balance that will bring harmony and well-being that serves our greatest potential.

Fire Spirit Is a Transformer

As we sit by the fireplace of the north, Fire Spirit transforms the energy bound up in the wood into heat, light, and smoke. With the breaking of old forms, the energy is released, freeing it up to create a new form. We feed the fire with our intent and our courage to move forward in our lives with greater awareness. We feed it our truth, and it burns brightly and lights the way.

We are offered new transformed energy with which to recreate our lives—a real, true, authentic, responsible, here's-who-I-am, here's-what-I-want kind of life.

At this point in the journey, we have a fuller understanding of our experiences and can begin the process of integrating them into the life we want to live, the life we have chosen. We embrace the change we have made and are grateful for our awakening. We know that east is right around the corner, and the circle of life continues. In the meantime, we will sit by the fire with our new awareness, knowing it is putting down a taproot inside us. This is wisdom.

Further Explorations of the North

C8 Choose one of the qualities associated with the north that
resonates with you: Transformer, wisdom keeper, spinner of
dreams, contemplative, accepting, nurturing, humble, vision.
Write that quality in your journal. Spend time with it—in other
words, just allow it to sit in your consciousness. You can go
out for a walk or sleep on it. When you feel ready, find a comfortable place where you can be uninterrupted for 30 minutes
or so. Close your eyes and place your hand over your heart.
Take several deep breaths and imagine your life with this
quality. Imagine yourself in a couple of typical experiences.
How do you feel when this quality is available and you are
expressing it? Where in your body does this quality resonate?
Breathe into it. Bring life to it. Ask yourself what stands in the
way of your fully embodying and experiencing this quality.
Write your response in your journal, being as specific as possible. Ask yourself if you are ready to let this block be healed.
Imagine what you will feel like when it is healed. Can you feel
that now? You can repeat this process with other qualities,
giving them time to take root in your heart, or you can focus
on the one you chose. Do what works best for you.

A Word About Confidentiality

Anything said in our group work is confidential; it stays in the
group room. Avoid talking about material outside of the circle. If you
have questions about confidentiality, ask your group leader or teacher.

Traversing the Three Realms of Consciousness

Whatever you can dream you can begin it.
Boldness has genius, and magic and power in it.
Begin it now.

~Goethe

As we walk through our Heart Reconnection journey, we are offered many realizations of how experience, belief, action, reaction, choice, and cause and effect all impact our lives and our interpretation of who we are. We are in the place of rediscovering the "I Am" of our life. As we do the work of looking deep into our life experience and our reflection into the world, we have the opportunity to see ourselves from more than one point of view. Having navigated the four directions of the medicine wheel this time around, we can view ourselves from the perspective of the three worlds of consciousness at any point on the wheel.

Right Here, Right Now

Our journey always begins in the *right here, right now* situations that drove us to this point of seeking healing. Whether we are turning to this book on our own for some guidance or with a group, a counselor, or as part of a treatment plan, we are opening up to the truth of what our life experience has become, and we are opening up to ideas for how we might live in joy and freedom.

We might label ourselves *bad, wrong, not good enough, sick, brokenhearted, angry, lost, self-destructive, defensive*—we may have lost balance, lost awareness, or lost faith in our authentic self and in life as a whole; we are all welcome in the medicine wheel. The calling card of awakening often comes as a train wreck of emotion.

The Three Worlds

Three aspects of consciousness are represented by three dimensions, or worlds. These realms are the Upper World (the realm of the Light, the Angels, and the Masters), the Middle World (our physical world here and now), and the Underworld (a place of conflict, heavy energy, challenges, temptations, and revelations). Our journey in this life begins with our place in the Middle World. This is our day-to-day past, present, and future. It is where we think, live, love, work, and interact. At the same time, the Middle World opens up to the shadows and darkness of the Underworld aspects of consciousness and life experience. It also opens up to the Upper World of light and the reflection of the whole of our being.

Despite the daily grind and the confusion and the fear, something greater than our current relationship to ourselves and our lives seems to be at work. The Great Mystery is moving in our lives. That is why we are here, in this place, right now. From the mundane of our Middle World life to the challenges of our Underworld consciousness, we are questioning, unraveling, and opening up parts of ourselves that have been closed off for years.

All of this is happening on all levels, all the time. Even though we may be absorbed in one aspect more than another, we are never not our whole being—we are never not all three aspects. We forget and become so involved in what we are all about that we lose awareness that we are of the light, that we are whole and perfect in the Upper World of human consciousness. This is the realm of the angels, the transcended ones, saints, great teachers, and holy ones. This aspect of our being is beyond the fears of not being good enough and being less than. In the light, we are at peace, aware, and awake. The feeling of this frequency of life is beyond words. We do our best to express our feelings, but words don't do this awareness justice.

The Middle World: Navigating the Physical Plane

The Middle World is the world into which we are born. It is defined by the physical plane. We are born into physical bodies with the aspects of being human—emotions, intellect, spirit, consciousness, form—all merged together into our unique human presence.

Living in this physical realm, we live by the nature of form and body, by our animal instincts as well as by the light of our spirit, and with the blessings and conflicts of our energetic inheritance. We live and die in this realm of the physical world.

On one hand, we have the amazing experience of being in this physical body, and on the other hand, dis-ease is a very present aspect of our physical existence, dis-ease of the body, dis-ease of the mind, and dis-ease of our soul. Our healing work first takes shape in the Middle World, as we seek to heal our own dis-ease. This is a critical aspect of rebalancing in this process of Heart Reconnection. Until we stop turning to whatever it is that keeps us from living life in balance—whether that's a behavior, drug, self-deprecating belief, judgment, identity label of "less than," and so on—we cannot reestablish the innate balance of our mind, body, and spirit.

In the Middle World, we work with our relationship to our body. As we address our physical aspects, we reclaim responsibility for our choices and shift our patterns, which shifts our energetic patterns, allowing us to avail ourselves of the energy to make new choices and create new supportive patterns. We also develop a practice of awareness of what is pushing our buttons and triggering our reactions. Living by reaction is an aspect of imbalance and dis-ease. Reactions are not choices; they are automatics that, if not checked and intervened on, will keep us trapped in cycles that no longer serve us.

Our baseline for healing is grounded in our Middle World relationships, as it is in our Middle World physical being that we can easily identify the symptoms of our dis-ease or imbalance. There is no judgment to this awareness. In fact, we can sit with finding gratitude for these physical manifestations that called us out to the light to find our way to healing. Suffering is, from a greater point of view, an invitation to come back to our core and own the cause and effect that's bringing suffering into our life. That way of relating to suffering makes suffering a gift, offering an awakening to our personal truth on a deeper level.

When we overidentify with our physical existence, we can fall into the sand trap of seeing ourselves as a victim of life's experiences. From one point of view, that can be true. Then again, from a greater point of view, we are simply the inheritors of the ways and experiences that were already in motion in this world, in our families, and in our communities before we were even born, and we just happen to be the one who inherited that experience in life. In that sense, our experience is not personal; it is simply life moving forward. Our response to these experiences becomes our legacy because we choose how we respond to our inherited experiences whether or not we are aware of making a choice.

While the world may say we are victims, our spirit may remind us that we are more than our existence in this world, and we hold the ability and power to heal these experiences and release that which has imprinted our DNA. We are the light, the spirit that brings life to our physical form; we are not limited to our physical form. Our ability to heal and evolve is our gift and responsibility to come to terms with.

This Middle World is the learning place, the life-practice place, the place of awakening. If we are to live the true offering of beauty and grace that can be our life's experience in this world, we must develop our own way to live a grounded life, here in our bodies, present in the moment, and with awareness of our wholeness. First, though, we usually need to deal with the realm of the Underworld.

Exploring the Middle World

1. On a new page in your journal, write your full name and, if possible, find a picture of yourself that you really like — maybe it's a picture of you as a child before you became bogged down with troubles or worries. Paste or tape the photo to that page, and then under the photo, write a commitment to yourself with regard to your Heart Reconnection journey.

2. Turn the page, skip the blank page on the back of your first page, and on the next page make a well-thought-out list of all the roles, labels, and identities you have taken on throughout your life, past and present. Do your best to list these without judgment. Emotions or feelings might come up as you think about these roles — that's fine, but just feel it and keep listing.

3. Once you have completed your list, sit with the energy of each of these roles and feel into what's there in relation to these various identities. Is there any old energy, fear, regret, pride, joy, sweetness, or bitterness? Practice sitting with what comes up and do your best to not go into any stories about it. Simply witness, breathe, and let it go. You can make notes of anything that feels noteworthy. This is a map of sorts of your life's path and the relationships you have invested yourself in along the way. The presence of old energies is a clue that you still hold an energetic investment in that role or story and you are still carrying it around with you. Ask yourself, *Is that what I want to do, really?*

4. Work this practice by reminding yourself not to go into judg-
    ment of any kind and simply be the witness to your reflec-
    tion. This is powerful, healing, and empowering. As you move
    through these roles, inhale deeply and blow out that old
    attachment on the exhale and say, "I release myself."

5. Repeat step 4 as many times as needed. Each time you do
    this, a little bit of the energetic attachments to your stories
    and roles is undone, and after a while, you will find that there
    is no energy left in those old stories. This is a way of clearing
    your Middle World reality; it's basic housekeeping.

6. If you wish, as a last step in this exercise, hold a fire cere-
    mony. Build a small fire in a fire pit. Tear the page or pages
    out of your notebook that you created in step 2. Give the
    paper and this practice to the fire where it can be recycled
    in the heavens. Release it with gratitude and without judg-
    ment (judgment keeps us attached so the release will not
    work). Every role and experience in life offers many angles
    and potential openings to our growth and evolution; see if
    you can find one gift in each of the roles or labels that you
    are ready to release. That shifts the practice from the Middle
    World to the Upper World, the realm of the angels and
    masters. Our willingness to let go of suffering frees our
    spirit and awareness to be more open to the presence of
    the higher realms.

The Underworld: Looking in the Mirror

The Underworld is a place of challenges, judgment, confusion, being lost and without direction, a lack of peace and security—all serving to call us out of what is familiar to us and back into the present moment, a place of awakening and realization of choice. Many of us wake up in the Underworld. We see our life as being out of control, painful, fearful, lost, and heartbroken. In the Underworld, we can no longer make sense of ourselves or our reality. Everything is twisted. We know something is very wrong, but we can't really sort it out clearly. Yes, maybe we drink too much or do too many drugs or act out in ways we know are destructive or life threatening, but even those actions seem unreal and inconsequential. We are deeply disconnected and lost in our own internal nightmare. *This* is the Underworld.

Once again, we are in a place of deep duality. On one hand, there is nothing good about it, *nothing*. But from a greater point of view, we are in a place that has gotten our attention through suffering and has called us out to take a long look in the mirror of life. Our pain and suffering, as tragic as they may be, are an invitation from life to pay attention. The Underworld offers challenges and trials that touch every aspect of our being. The conflict is real and runs throughout our entire being. The heart begs, "Please, don't do that anymore!" but the mind and body scream for relief from the pain. In this place, we are in deep; we are lost, spinning, afraid, angry, and desperate. We are still no less the amazing beings we are at our core, but we are in a place of intense conflict, delusion, and cause-and-effect reality.

After having fed our patterns for so long, those patterns hold more of our energy than what we have available to just say no. Our physical body is addicted in a physical sense, and our emotional body—our mind—is addicted in an energetic sense. We have clung to our fixes for so long that we have lost a sense of self without them. We can't remember how it felt before we were addicted. This twisted, energetic, emotional, physiological realm is a hell of sorts. We are lost in an internal turmoil from which we seem to have no way out.

In the Underworld, there is no baseline for reality checks. There is no way out from the same ways of living and believing that got us here in the first place. The Underworld is a place of reckoning. We are faced with the full reality of our past manifesting in the overwhelming present state and the invitations of the moment to see through the shrouds and clouds of confusion, looking for a glimmer of another possible choice. We are confronted with all our stuff and still, if only in brief flashes, shown the opening to a life of something else.

We must make choices in this Underworld realm, as to make no choice is to choose the misery we have known. There is no going back from here. There is no recovering how we used to be; that is done, in and of the past. To learn our way around our soul-searching place, the Underworld offers us a reconnection to the deeper aspects of ourselves that we have never lost but have clearly turned away from. We no longer know ourselves, yet who we are really is still here within.

The Underworld place is a journey. We do not simply decide we have healed completely and walk out. That's a shallow approach to the great offerings of the Underworld. The greatest gifts of having fallen so deep into our own mess is that we learn about the power of our heart, the resilience of our minds, and the ability of our body to heal. We learn the lessons of the great imbalance as we unravel ourselves and reconnect to our heart. There is no hurry, as this is not a scorecard process. No scorecard can grant us a release from our Underworld challenge. Push too hard and we might go on living free of our coping mechanisms but still feel conflicted, insecure, egotistical, and angry.

Respecting our journey offers us the lesson of patience. Patience is a bad-tasting medicine at first, but it is a lifesaver once we develop a taste for it. The great work of Heart Reconnection begins in an Underworld consciousness, and we recreate our way back toward the realm of the Upper World, one day, one move, and one choice at a time. Once again, we are working beyond the limitations of the mind's attachments to judgment. We are not keeping a score as right or wrong, good or bad. We are fostering an openhearted relationship to change. This relationship is based in simple action and reaction, cause and effect. We get what we get and give what we give, and the outcomes are our result, plain and simple. This requires great practice and a lot of reframing our experiences, and why not?

We are living with the great unknown of life in an in-between-the-worlds place. We can know we do not want what we have been living as our way in life any longer, but we have no real sense of what life on the other side of this Underworld place can be. The invitation is to learn to let go, and let go, and let go, and take small steps forward, intent on each choice and move, realizing that we are loaded with the habit of living by reactions to life and learning to intervene on our ingrained patterns of reaction. We are an apprentice to a new awareness of life, self, heart, and spirit.

Remember, this is not a race; this is a recreation of our relationship to ourselves and to life. Through practice, we wean our mind off of judgment as our relative status measure, and we start living by choice and action, letting each response go. This undoes our old way of creating more baggage in life and more of the poison of judging ourselves at every turn. We live one day, breath, choose, and move at a time and with grace.

Exploring the Underworld

1. In your journal, on the top of a clean page, write Underworld—The Blessings of Waking Up. Beneath that heading, make a list of the challenges you know you are facing in your life. These can be behaviors, addictions, relationships to a toxic person, fears, resentments, trauma, the loss of a role or relationship—basically anything you know is haunting you and undermining your ability to feel free and happy.

2. Write down whatever comes to your mind as a reflection on your relationship with the challenges on your list. How does your enmeshment with these challenges make you feel? Express this.

3. After you reflect on each one, take a moment to breathe deeply and release your attachment to what you just wrote. This is the beginning of a practice to separate who you are from the energies of the roles, labels, and behaviors you have become enmeshed with. Remember, even though you may not believe it yet, *you are not what you do or have done.* Those things are the experiences and choices of our lives; they may define what we have created as our frame of life, but they *do not define who we are as human beings.*

4. After you have written out your list and your reflections, come back to each aspect and sit with it: what are the gifts or possible gifts that can come from your relationship to the things you have identified? What more might be revealed? If you were to dream beyond this shadow place, how might you

imagine your challenges becoming openings to blessings?
Write this down. Again, sit with it, use your imagination, and
listen to your heart. If nothing comes, that's fine too; you can
come back later and revisit this list. That's the beauty of the
journey around the medicine wheel; we always come back
around to revisit our perspective. From our heart-centered
place, we will eventually find the gifts that came through our
suffering; however small they may seem, any opening to the
light is a good one, and as we learn to live toward the light of
awareness, our life will grow open and aware of the power we
hold within ourselves to recreate our experience with ourselves and in our world. The Underworld can be ruthless and
cold, and the Underworld calls out the best in us if we are to
unravel our enmeshment with its shadows and fears. We are
greater than our challenges, and we are worthy of the time
and energy to free ourselves from all of that that does not
serve us.

The Realm of the Upper World: Shifting to a Sense of Peace

The Upper World is the realm of the spirit people, the angels, and
the masters. This realm is beyond what we know as judgment, fear,
and insecurity. The Upper World represents the qualities of vision,
expansion, far seeing, big picture, and infinity. It expands our thinking, enlarges our vision, raises our expectations and understanding
of ourselves, and encourages us to reach for the stars. That doesn't
exclude working hard for our vision, but it assures us that it can
happen.

Early on in one's healing journey, there's talk about being on a "pink cloud" and warnings that the pink cloud is not real and won't last. Let's consider this for a moment: what if that pink cloud is the presence of our whole true self, our spirit, our Upper World consciousness coming forward as a result of our stepping up into the present moment? We have let go of the suffering and insanity of chaos that had become our reality, and for the first time in a long time, we are feeling our spirit.

The contrast is so amazing between fear, chaos, and guilt and this calm, at peace, "it's-all-really-okay-and-I-am-really-okay" awareness that we are just happy, grateful, and content to be right here, right now. Is this wrong? Is this feeling *real*? Yes, of course the feeling is real, and the truth is that our attention has shifted from what had been so familiar—fear and suffering—to a deep abiding sense of peace that we are lit up with gratitude and sweetness.

With that said, the reality is also that energy tends to follow its patterns, and more than likely our attention will once again be hooked by old experiences, drama, and the challenges that lie ahead, and we will lose our Upper World consciousness to the ways of the Middle World and even the Underworld. Nevertheless, this entire experience is a beautiful gift that has revealed to us that there are many states of being, all existing within us all the time.

We will experience the particular state or frequency of mind, thought, and belief to which we happen to choose to give our attention. If we give our attention to fear, we feel fear. If we give our attention to frustration or anger, we feel and experience that frequency in our bodies and emotions. If we give our attention to gratitude, grace, and joy for the moment, we will experience the feeling of happiness and gratitude as a frequency of life moving through us. This is all occurring by the nature of what we give our attention to and how aware and responsible we are in directing our own attention.

Our pink cloud is a frequency of life just as drama and fear are frequencies of life. When we live from a shallow or unawakened awareness of life, we do not practice directing and being responsible for directing our attention, so we get hooked by whatever pops up in the moment. Like a whack-a-mole game, thoughts, reactions, and outside situations pop up, and our attention automatically goes there. We are not owning what we are giving our attention to; we are being hooked and dragged into whatever is going on in or around us. Culturally, we are not taught to direct our attention and be aware of the reactions that come up so that we are living with awareness of our feelings and reactions moment to moment. A life lived in reaction is not a life lived by conscious choice. Conscious choice is intentional; there is an awareness of what we are doing and why, and we take responsibility for each choice. In reaction, we respond without responsibility for what we are giving energy to; we just go there and—*boom!*

From an Upper World perspective, living life by awareness, taking responsibility for each response, and feeling and owning each emotion, thought, and move in life—this is a life lived by intent and with the clarity of the angels. We do not fall into judgment or fear of outcomes. We live in the moment with intention and in alignment with our heart and spirit. This doesn't mean things always go our way or we always get what we want. It does mean we do not live in reaction to how life rolls. Rather, we live in conscious choice. This saves us from making a bad situation worse by pouring gasoline on a fire. We live awake and aware and in the flow of our moment-to-moment experience. This is acceptance at its highest. While we still have excitement and disappointment, heartbreak and happiness, we do not lose ourselves to these feelings or at least not for long. We are aware that all life is passing through and nothing is forever.

From the Upper World, we are offered a connection to the freedom from bondage to humanity's ways on earth, the freedom from demanding outcomes or fearing failure. If we find ourselves on a pink cloud, so be it. That cloud is as real as we choose to make it, and with practice, we might just learn a new way of living, inspired by the experience of love and freedom that came from our pink cloud. After all, we are the light, not the shadows we cast into the world.

Exploring the Upper World

- ❧ In your journal, begin a thread of reflection in which you identify and acknowledge the blessings in your day-to-day life. Keeping this journal will shift your attention from keeping "score" to being a witness. There is no place for judgment here, just an awareness of your daily interactions. At the end of each day for at least a month, walk back through your day's interactions in your mind and write down each experience you recognize as a blessing or gift. Whether you were the receiver or the one giving the gift, acknowledge both equally. We cannot give what we do not have, so know that if you are receiving gifts, you are also extending them.

- ❧ Each time you go outside during the day, stop for a moment, close your eyes, and turn your face up to the sun. With all your awareness, breathe in the light of the sun. Breathe in deeply and slowly. As you inhale, feel the light moving through your entire body and being. As you exhale, let go of conflicts, challenges, day-to-day fears, etc. Simply allow your whole being to become the light. By shifting your attention to the light and merging with the light, you are raising your frequency, clearing your energy body, calming your physical body, and easing your mind. As you shift into the light, if you are inclined, ask your angels and guides to be with you. Give this practice a try for a month and see what comes to you. Have faith as you develop patience with yourself and with how life unfolds for you when you show up for yourself.

In our heart and soul, we are all related by the spirit of life itself, flowing through us and throughout creation. Maybe this is a dance, maybe a journey, maybe a practice, maybe a ritual—call it what you will, the words are not what's important. Regardless of what is still left to do, we allow ourselves to feel the depth of the progress we've made. We honor and humble ourselves, and we feel grateful. We understand intuitively that love is what matters most. The root of human suffering is the belief that something is wrong with us, that we are not worthy of love. Learning to love is the journey.

Conclusion

Go confidently in the direction of your dreams.
Live the life you've imagined.

~Henry David Thoreau

We are born into this world as inheritors of the legacies of being a human, each of us born of the light of consciousness merged with the form of our human body, each of us a unique expression of the one that created us—God, the Mystery, the Great Spirit, Life—flowing through us from the moment of conception until we release our physical form and return to source of all that is.

Who am I? Who are you? Where do we come from? To where do we return? These are questions of existence, purpose, reason, and faith. The truth is that there are many, many beliefs across the spectrum of humanity concerning our existence, where we come from, and where we might ultimately go when we depart this world. Who of us can know for certain? We cannot answer those questions for a fact. We can only know for certain that "I am here. I am alive in this realm of birth, life, and death."

Living in this world of duality—light and dark, male and female, up and down, in and out—it is clear we have more questions than absolute answers. If we each were to describe what we believe, we must qualify our story as that which is not absolute facts or knowing, but rather a belief taught, inherited, experienced, or imagined. This is the amazing mystery of life on earth: we are here without an absolute knowing of before or after, and still we are here, alive and experiencing each moment and each breath, each feeling and choice.

If you've been traversing the wheel, you know that this Heart Reconnection journey is a journey we take over and over again. With each pass around the wheel, we gain new insights and greater awareness. Every day is a new day. We are not the same person we were yesterday or last month or last year. Heart Reconnection is a process of continuously asking, "Who am I?" and "What am I doing?" We are stepping into owning our life from a place of responsibility, gratitude, respect, and authenticity. There's no need to live our life from a place of seeking validation and trying to be good enough. Our only need is to live an authentic life connected to our heart and guided by our personal truth.

Closing Ritual

Occasionally in life there are those moments
of unutterable fulfillment, which cannot be completely
explained by those symbols called words.
Their meanings can only be articulated by the
inaudible language of the heart.

~Martin Luther King Jr.

As you stand in the heart of the medicine wheel, you are standing in your own heart space. Take a few deep breaths and feel the ground beneath your feet. Earth is your mother; she took you by the hand when you entered the wheel, and she walked the journey with you. It is her heart that you feel beating inside of you just as you felt your mother's heart when she carried you inside her body.

Turn slowly and look deeply into each of the directions. You have created a place within you of love, forgiveness, compassion, healing, kindness, generosity, courage, and acceptance. Place your hand over your heart and slowly walk around the wheel, pausing at each of the directions marking your journey and offering gratitude. Spend time

125

in the center, letting the insights and healing of the four directions come together in your heart.

When you feel that you have completed your journey for this time around the wheel, begin in the north and walk slowly to the west, to the south, and to the east, closing the wheel.

There is often a hesitation at the end of a powerful experience such as the medicine wheel journey. We naturally want to prolong these feelings. Your feelings are deep, and that is beautiful. At the same time, your life of reconnection awaits you.

Teacher's Guide to Heart Reconnection Therapy (HRT)

In a futile attempt to erase our past, we deprive the
community of our healing gift. If we conceal our wounds
out of fear and shame, our inner darkness can neither
be illuminated nor become a light for others.

~Brennan Manning, Abba's Child:
The Cry of the Heart for Intimate Belonging

I. Introduction to the Teacher's Guide

As humans, we long for connection with our deepest self. We long to become familiar with our very essence, to know our deepest truths, and to understand what influences the decisions we make. As we begin the journey of reconnecting with our deepest and most sacred self, it's helpful to seek wisdom and guidance to show us how to make it through to the other side.

Some of us get lost along the way. Others of us temporarily lose our confidence and need help so that we may find our strength again. We learn that empowerment, love, and a safe place where we can connect, support, and encourage one another as we create the life we were meant to live are possible.

To transform our lives, we need to change our stories, moving beyond the limitations of own mind and return to our true self. This section of this book is a teacher's guide to the Heart Reconnection journey of waking up to the reality that we are responsible for the life we live, responsible for who we really are, and responsible for becoming an active participant in our own lives instead of a bystander.

The expression "If nothing changes, nothing changes" beautifully illustrates how desire alone does not promote change. It's a good start but that's all it is—a good start. Living from the heart requires that we tap back into that part of us that recognizes and is ready to remember, reconnect, and take action.

We are all creative. Somewhere along the line many of us disconnected from that part of ourselves and began believing something different, something that limited who we are and who we want to be. Creativity and its expression is a most effective tool for psychological growth and healing. When we call up our creativity in all its many glorious forms, we become more aware of our beliefs, thoughts, and feelings, along with the *felt sense* experience we carry inside of us (*felt sense* describes internal bodily awareness of emotion, intuition, awareness, and embodiment). Creativity reconnects us with our heart and the "still small voice within." So affirm your creative nature and read on! This is the action part of the change process. The part where you move from desire to practicing new ways of living that will reconnect you to your heart.

NOTE: You may choose to do the work in this teacher's guide with a therapist if you're reading this book on your own or find a group of like-minded adventurers who are ready to step into their own healing process with you. This teacher's guide along with the main body of the book are not intended as a substitute for professional treatment. If you need help, we encourage you to seek the advice of a professional mental health practitioner. Some of the exercises in the teacher's guide may bring up discomfort. If so, it's important to have trusted people to hold space for you as you work through the discomfort.

II. HRT Principles

Heart Reconnection Therapy (HRT) is a process for healing from anything that keeps a person from accessing their ability to heal and thrive. Below the brokenness and the attempts to avoid the pain, all beings are whole and perfect. Healing is about restoring that sense of self. Heart Reconnection Therapy is deeper and more comprehensive than treatment. Treatment applies protocols and formulas in a pre-determined program. Heart Reconnection Therapy is personal and transformational. It involves many levels of healing, making deep changes that affect all areas of one's life. The heart holds the truth of who we are when the authentic self is allowed to emerge.

Heart Reconnection Therapy evolved as a group of us with life-times of experience in the field of recovery sat around a table in Santa Fe, New Mexico, sharing concerns about addiction and treatment. We were puzzled by the low success rate of treatment that, despite the proliferation of facilities across the country, new studies on the brain, and the emergence of evidence-based practices, persists in hovering around 25 percent.

Our goal was to identify healing processes that we knew from experience were the most helpful and, by combining efforts, develop a new program and perhaps a new paradigm for working with people who have addiction. Our goal quickly expanded to include people who have experienced trauma or are struggling with any other conditions that keep them from moving forward in their lives. We wanted more people to succeed in their recovery efforts and experience the freedom and joy that we know is on the other side of the struggle.

Treatment facilities have been known to place blame on the client when treatment doesn't yield the expected results. Rather than focusing on the client as the problem, our focus was on improving the care people receive as a way of yielding better results. With a 75 percent failure rate, we knew that the need wasn't for more of the same; it was for an approach that was broader and deeper. We stepped off the well-worn trail and explored new territory. We looked at practices we knew from experience were effective, and we placed them on a path of awakening that looks at people in the light of their innate wholeness rather than in their brokenness.

Heart Reconnection Therapy's protocols are substantially different from treating addiction, trauma, and the accompanying conditions separately. The difference exists in our beliefs and agreements that inform the way treatment is presented as well as what treatment is presented. We have a core understanding that the ability to heal is inherent to the human condition and that people heal best in climates of affirmation, connection, respect, and community. These qualities set the tone of Heart Reconnection Therapy.

Attention is given to creating and maintaining emotional safety throughout the Heart Reconnection experience and all aspects of the program. HRT's timetable and protocols align with each person's individual needs. People on the Heart Reconnection journey are not viewed as addicts, alcoholics, trauma victims, or any of the other wounds/labels acquired in life. Rather, they are simply people who seek healing and connection. Identity based on wounds gives too much power to the condition.

To reframe the addictive urge, consider the following questions, noticing their impact:

- What if we let go of overpathologizing addictive urges and all the other coping mechanisms?
- What if these urges aren't character defects, but instead symptoms of a deeply spiritual, if unconscious, impulse to awaken to our true self, our own good heart, and our place in the natural world?
- What if the state of mind to which we have become accustomed is not representative of our true nature, but is an altered state induced by culture and circumstances?
- What would it be like if there was nothing intrinsically wrong with any of us?
- What if we looked deeper into a person beyond the behaviors and saw them at the level of the heart?
- What if the time-honored ceremonial practices of indigenous cultures, which allow transformative states of consciousness, connected participants to something beyond conditioned thought patterns?
- What if the urge to escape is actually a yearning to return to our own unique truth and to the vitality we experience while lying on our backs beneath a night sky?
- What if our current crisis is actually nature calling us home to her and, at some level, we know that we cannot rest until we make that return?

- What if a central task of Heart Reconnection Therapy is to create experiences that support such a return to the heart within us, in our relationships, and in our relationship to the natural world?

Notice the absence of shame and how these questions evoke compassion.

Heart Reconnection Therapy encourages good relations as a primary healing protocol for healing the wounded heart. This practice often begins with simple kindnesses extended to one other, and quickly translates to an improved self-to-self relationship. In the environment of compassion, people find safety and are able to lower their defenses. This is when healing begins.

Nature and Play Are at the Heart of Heart Reconnection Therapy

Nature is foundational to Heart Reconnection Therapy. Every element in a human body is found in the earth itself; we are integrally earth creatures. Our mind can forget the importance of this connection, but our body remembers itself in nature. It seeks reconnection with the earth and with plants, and animals, and birds, and all the other creatures. We crave this connection for physical and mental balance. Our internal clock is still geared to sunrise and sunset, to the seasons of the year, the rhythm of the tide and the flow of the river as it winds sensuously across the meadow on its way to the sea. Without these vital connections we drift off course, we begin to accept artificiality as the real thing, and we self-medicate. Nature puts us right!

In Joan Borysenko's decade of experience directing mind-body clinics at a Harvard teaching hospital, she realized how in addition to laughter, bonding, and play, a single hour-long silent walk in nature could open a window that leads straight to the heart. Halfway through a 10-week program that taught meditation, mindfulness, forgiveness, emotional literacy, and yoga—creating a safe space for deep sharing and the emergence of authentic community—there was a full-day Sunday session. Like a mother hen, Joan would lead twenty or so of her chicks across busy city streets to a greenbelt that ran for miles along Boston's Muddy River. Traffic sounds receded as Mother Earth enfolded even the most reluctant participant in her web of enchantment.

The beauty and evanescence of a raindrop, the sparkling wake left by a cruising duck, the fat, smooth roots of giant beech trees—"How could it be that I've never actually seen these things before?" That was the almost universal refrain. Faces softened, hearts opened, and unexpected seeds of healing took root. The ragtag group that walked back to the hospital was palpably different than the one that had crossed the busy street just an hour before.

Nature, whether we're alone on an extended vision quest or walking through an inner city green space, is one of many portals to greater wisdom and to our heart. Willing or unwilling, Nature works her magic with and through us. As psychiatrist Carl Jung carved above the door to his home in Zurich, *"Vocatus atque non vocatus deus aderit."* This Latin phrase means, "Called or not called, God is present." And nowhere is that nonlocal, eternal presence—whatever you choose to call it—more universally accessible than in nature and in play.

Therefore, Heart Reconnection Therapy calls for as much time outside as the weather allows, and sometimes despite the weather. HRT therapists have been known to accompany groups out into a warm spring rain to smell it, hear it, and feel it running down our faces and dripping off our noses. Sophistication dissolves and a genuine little kid emerges, laughing and splashing in puddles.

> You can discover more about a person in an hour
> of play than in a year of conversation.
>
> ~Plato

III. HRT Teachings and Practices

In addition to leading clients, individually or as a group, through the medicine wheel exploration activities in the main body of this book, the following teachings and practices are intended to empower clients and bring about healing and sustainable well-being.

These practices do not have to be done in order, though it may make sense to perform certain practices in sequence. As the group leader or individual counselor, read through all of these practices and take your clients on various practices in the Heart Reconnection journey as you feel they are ready for them.

Make these practices yours by using wording that feels most comfortable and natural to you. The majority of these practices address the participant directly, so you can also use the many of the practices verbatim in your groups and individual sessions if you'd like.

Topic: Return to the Great Mystery

The Invitation: What does it mean to return to the Great Mystery and reconnect with your heart? We invite you to begin your Heart Reconnection journey by first creating sacred space for the work and journaling throughout your journey. What follows are some practices for creating sacred space and ways in which to record your experiences.

The Teaching: Humans have been creating sacred spaces that create connection since the beginning of time. American mythologist Joseph Campbell said that sacred space is where you can find yourself again and again. The desire to create sacred space is so deep within the soul that we tend to create this space unconsciously.

Think about your own space. Do you have pictures of family and friends on a table or mantle? A place for mementos from a favorite trip? An altar with candles, stones, or flowers? A garden you love and take pleasure from?

Creating an environment where healing can take place is key to Heart Reconnection work. As the poet Rumi says, "Everything that you want, you already are." Looking inward lays the foundation for healing to happen and encourages you to set an intention for the work you are doing.

Teacher, we encourage you to start each group or individual session with one or more of the following practices:

- **Smudging**—Smudging is a practice that purifies and cleanses one's energy field. It also creates sacred space for the group and offers a way to leave the energy of the outside world outside. Using a feather and a bundle of sage (smudge stick) held over a flame-retardant bowl, smudge yourself by lighting the sage and using the feather to gently direct the smoke toward you, starting with your head and moving down the body clockwise.

  If in a group, one person can start the smudging practice by turning to the person on their right and directing the sage smoke toward that person with the feather, starting at the bottom of the chin and moving around the face clockwise.

Ask the person to extend their arms out to the side and smudge from the neck over the right arm, to the hand and back (under the arm), to the chest and over the left arm, returning to the chest (under the arm). Moving down the body, smudge the torso, move down the right leg, and then down the left leg. Stand upright, gently touching the person's left arm so that they know to put their arms down to the sides.

Have the person turn clockwise and smudge in a horizontal zigzag pattern starting with the head, down the body, and back up. Ask the person to turn back toward you and hand them the smudge stick, bowl, and feather so that they can now smudge the person to their right. The items are passed from person to person until the original "smudger" has been smudged.

- **Create an altar**—The practice of creating sacred space through altars has been around for thousands of years. An altar can provide a focal point that reminds us to reconnect with the spiritual place in our heart. Altars can be simple or more elaborate, for general or more specific purposes. To use an altar to start a group or an individual session, invite client(s) to bring a small representative item with them and set an intention for the session by placing that item on the altar to represent their intention. Initially, you may want to have items available such as stones, crystals, flowers, and small pictures and then encourage the clients in an ongoing group to bring something of their own for the altar next time. You may light incense and/or a candle to signal the setting of intentions and/or the start of group.

- **A moment of silence and intention setting**—Start the group or session with a period of silence or meditation to allow all in attendance to connect with their heart and the divine and to set an intention for this part of the journey on which each individual is about to embark on. You may include a nondenominational prayer for blessings as well.

- **Releasing**—On a small slip of paper, each individual can write down anything they are holding on to and want to let go of so that it doesn't interfere with the work that is about to take place. As each person silently expresses gratitude for the lessons they've learned because of these things, the paper is placed on the altar and consciously released. If a "burning bowl" is available, burn the paper; make sure the bowl is flame retardant. (See the practice on page 138–139.)

- **Making a commitment to hold space**—Have the group form a circle. A meaningful, sacred object can be placed in the middle of the circle or in a prominent place. Invite each group member to place a personal object in the circle as a commitment to holding space for the group members. Have each member of the group select a cloth (such as scarves or pieces of different colored fabrics). Ask each member to state a commitment to holding space for themselves and other group members and place their cloth in front of them (laying it out so that the cloth connects with the person's cloth beside them and eventually forms a circle).

  After each member has shared their commitment, say the following: "Each of us has made a commitment to hold space for ourselves and others in this group in their Heart Reconnection journey. If you are willing to further commit to holding this space without judgment, shaming, fixing, or disengaging, and agree to offer unconditional support with an open heart, please step over your cloth and say, 'I commit to this.'"

→ **Practice: Sacred Space Guided Meditation**

Teacher, recite the following to lead others or record the script and play back. Do not say the numerals aloud; they are only included as a guide. Be sure to allow enough time for each step to be implemented before going on to the next step.

1. *Sit or lie down in a comfortable position.*

2. *Gently close your eyes and take a few deep breaths from the belly . . . (pause)*

3. *With each exhalation, feel your body relax more and more . . . (pause)*

4. *Now take a few more deep breaths and feel your mind relax along with your body . . . slowing down your thoughts and just noticing these thoughts floating by easily and effortlessly . . . (pause) allowing your mind to let go of any particular focus and turning inward to that deep place within you that desires healing . . . (pause)*

5. *Now imagine a place in nature where you feel at peace, at ease and a sense of well-being . . . (long pause)*

6. *Look around you and notice what you see in your sacred space . . . using all of your senses . . . notice the colors, the smells, the sounds, the feel of the elements beneath and around you . . . (pause)*

7. *And as you see yourself in this space, imagine that there is a presence within you and all around you that is loving . . . and kind . . . and compassionate . . . (pause)*

8. *Notice that this presence permeates the space you are in and is nurturing you, caring for you, protecting you and guiding you . . . (pause)*

9. *Feel this presence... know this presence... trust this presence ... and as you do, know that it is with you always... (pause)*

10. *Take a few moments and just enjoy the feeling... the felt sense... of being in your sacred space and taken care of completely by the universe... (pause)*

11. *When you're ready, bring your awareness back in to the present moment and share the felt sense experience you had with the group from the feeling level.*

Topic: Journaling in the Heart Reconnection Journey

The Teaching: The value of journaling in the Heart Reconnection process cannot be underestimated. The value is not necessarily in what is written but in having a record of personal recollections of one's innermost thoughts throughout the Heart Reconnection journey. Journaling provides a vehicle for conscious examination of the unconscious processes that come to light along the way, and using a journal to record your journey is strongly recommended.

The repetition of recording your experiences in whatever way you choose allows for greater personal understanding during and after this journey. Journal consistently throughout the Heart Reconnection process, and journaling will become an automatic vehicle through which you begin to bring the unconscious to the light and discern what is of most significance in your life so that you may change your story.

Here's how to make the most of journaling throughout this journey and all others:

1. **Decide which journal medium you will use.** There are several mediums to choose from—digital, pen and paper, visual, or aural. The important thing is to choose a journal medium you are comfortable with and inspires you to write, as you will be asking yourself a lot of questions during this journey. (Regardless of the type of journal you use, the prompts in these practices will say to write your responses; if you are speaking yours, just replace the word "write" with "respond.") Reflecting on the questions and answers you come up with makes it easier to understand and gain insights, which often makes the healing process easier. It's important to remember, however, that one must not always understand before healing happens.

   If you decide to use pen and paper, purchase a new notebook or journal so that you can start fresh. Using a pen that feels good in your hand can provide a psychological boost during the writing process.

   An audio journal is helpful for those who prefer talking or processing out loud rather than writing. There are voice recorder apps available for smartphone or computer or digital recorders that you can carry with you and upload your recordings later if you don't have a smartphone.

   If you prefer electronics, journaling on your computer or phone is an option. You may decide to keep an online journal and share your experiences by blogging as you make the journey. You may or may not share the link with others, but the commitment you make to post regularly may help keep you accountable.

   Research suggests that art expression may help us reconnect our thinking and feeling and subsequently connect implicit (felt sense) and explicit (narrative) memories. Visual journaling is a way to record our inner world or the "felt-sense knowing" that lies just below the surface of our awareness that we don't have words for yet. The 2009 publication of *The Red Book* (Carl Jung's visual images and text) is considered by many to be the classic example of visual journaling. Drawing, painting, "doodling," or making things in general allows us to not just think differently, but to *feel* differently as well.

2. **Take the time to examine your thoughts, feelings, and the actions you engage in response.** As you reflect and write about these things, question what you did, looking for themes, habits, and patterns in your answers. Doing so begins to prepare you to rewrite your story.

3. **Be creative.** Remember that creativity is a wellness practice and can decrease depressive symptoms, increase positive emotions, reduce stress responses, and, in some cases, improve immune system functioning.

4. **Read your journal regularly.** Take time to reflect on the things you've written, looking for themes and patterns, and evaluating progress you've made.

Questions to Contemplate:

To begin the Heart Reconnection process, here are some questions to contemplate and begin to answer:

- Who are you, really?
- How well do you know yourself?
- Why are you here?
- What is your heart's desire?

- What, if anything, stops you from pursuing your heart's desire?
- What truth is your heart longing to speak?
- What would you do if you loved yourself unconditionally? How can you act on these things whether you do or don't?
- What do you feel like you need to know right away?
- Do you believe in something greater than you such as a Higher Power, Spirit, or Source? If so, describe the nature of this power and your relationship with it.

Topic: The Medicine Wheel

The Teaching: The medicine wheel as it's used in this book is representative of Native American spirituality. Within the medicine wheel are the four directions and the four sacred colors. The circle represents the circle of life (including the four aspects of self) and is never ending, life without end. The medicine wheel is used to provide guidance and direction for understanding the journey of life and to assist in achieving well-being. It symbolizes the individual journey that each us must take to find our own path and teaches us that all lessons, all talents, and all abilities are equal. Movement in the wheel is circular and typically in a clockwise, or "sun-wise" direction. This helps to align with the forces of nature, such as gravity and the rising and setting of the sun.

There is no one universal version of the wheel and many ways to use it. We use the wheel as a framework to represent an integrative, complete picture of the self, and encourage that it be used to create a map of sorts for enhancing awareness and creating change.

→ Practice: Making a Medicine Wheel

1. Pick a place that is meaningful to you. It can be a table, an altar, or the floor.

2. Take a moment and say a prayer for the medicine wheel to change your life, to heal, to protect you, and to create sacred space.

3. Find objects or use objects that are sacred or meaningful to you. They could be stones, crystals, animal fetishes, shells, etc. Get a compass and find the directions. Place your hand in the east and think about the qualities of the east discussed in chapter 6. Select one of your objects that reflects these qualities and place in on the wheel in the direction of the east. Moving clockwise, repeat this exercise for each direction (see chapters 7, 8, and 9).

4. The center of the circle is your life. Think about your spiritual center, who helps you and guides you, and let one of your objects call you, then place it in the center.

5. Close your eyes, bless the medicine wheel, and ask it to help you change your life.

→ Practice: Medicine Bag

Traditionally, a medicine bag holds within it sacred objects that bring about healing. For this practice, begin with a pouch or a cloth in which you will place your chosen objects. Look over the qualities listed at the beginning of the chapters for each of the four directions (see chapters 6, 7, 8, and 9).

Choose an object that represents your relationship to all the values of the east, one for the values of the south, one for the values of the west, and one for the values of the north. Then, choose an object that represents whatever else is relevant in your life today, such as the most important relationships you're currently in. Place those objects in your pouch.

Then, three times a week or so, remove all the objects from the pouch, spread them out in front of you, and then choose the relationship you want to explore. Hold the object, and using your imagination, breathe with the object as if you are breathing into it. Connect to it.

Allow yourself to enter into the frequency of that relationship as it exists within you. Sit with it—not from a place of expectation or even intention but as a witness to what might be revealed to you. Without judgment, be fully aware of what comes: What feelings come up? What thoughts wander through? What sensations do you experience? Journal your insights, impressions, thoughts, and questions.

Topic: Finding and Speaking Your Truth

The Teaching: Bruce Lipton, PhD, a cell biologist and former Stanford research scholar, studies and writes about the impact of our thoughts on our cells. In a video interview, he says, "Before we blame the cells, we must first look at our thoughts, our beliefs, and our behaviors because these are more important to our health than the genes." He concludes, "When we change our thoughts, behaviors, and beliefs, we can change our biology. We are the masters of our lives not the victim of our genes."[3]

What are the wounds and beliefs that have silenced the wisdom of the heart? The programming we absorbed as children and continue to

---

3 *https://www.brucelipton.com/resource/video-and-podcasts/bruce-h-lipton-phd-paris-the-impact-our-environment-and-our-state-mind.*

believe as adults gets in the way of our true self shining through. What is a belief? A belief is simply a statement that we have accepted as true. We have stored away in our subconscious mind a set of beliefs about ourselves that perpetuate the negative core beliefs that are in operation when we feel most stuck and hopeless about our lives. Author and lecturer Earnie Larsen calls these negative beliefs the "old lies."

It's time to decide: are you going to continue to believe the lies or is it time to change your belief system and heal the wounds that have silenced your heart? As you step on this path of transformation, affirm your decision to accept yourself completely, just as you are, and release the old lies and self-limiting stories. Reach out and ask for the support you need to create new truths that support and encourage the beauty and awesomeness of your true self.

→ Practice: Identify Old Lies and Create New Truths

Before getting started, ground yourself by taking five deep breaths. Feel your feet on the ground and find a place inside of you that feels solid, centered, grounded, and connected. When you're ready, copy the following in your journal:

TRIGGERING EXPERIENCE/EVENT/SITUATION:			
AUTOMATIC NEGATIVE THOUGHT	I FELT	WHAT I DID (BEHAVIOR)	RESULTS

NEGATIVE CORE BELIEF:

Now identify several events or situations (using the above format for each event/situation you identify) that happened when you were young that were painful and triggered (created or led to) negative thoughts, feelings, and actions. The negative thoughts will be things your critical voice says to you when you have been triggered by an event or situation. This voice reflects the negative core beliefs (old lies) you accepted as truth somewhere along the line. Here is an example to get you started:

TRIGGERING EXPERIENCE/EVENT/SITUATION:
My father was helping me with my math homework and when I couldn't figure out how to get the right answer he told me I would never pass third grade.

AUTOMATIC NEGATIVE THOUGHT	I FELT	WHAT I DID (BEHAVIOR)	RESULTS
"I hate him"	Anger	Started crying	Got spanked
"I'll never get it"	Fear	Pretended I understood	Failed test

"I'm stupid"	Shame	Pretended I didn't care	Felt alone

NEGATIVE CORE BELIEF:

Negative Core Belief is "I'm stupid."

Identifying where your negative core beliefs came from, and how they got so strong through years of practice, is a good beginning to start changing them and creating new truths upon which to live your life. Look at your list and ask yourself, "Do I see how this belief came about?" Next, identify what you would like to believe about yourself (your new truth) as you read each statement on your list. Here is an example:

NEGATIVE CORE BELIEF	NEW TRUTH
I AM STUPID.	I AM COMPETENT AND CAPABLE.
I AM UNLOVABLE.	I AM PRECIOUS.
I AM DAMAGED.	I AM WHOLE AND GOOD.

Practice the new beliefs that are aligned with what you want (the new truths) by affirming them repeatedly out loud or in writing. You can record yourself stating your new truths and listen to the recording as well. The key is to go beyond just saying it. You want to really lean into this new belief and *feel* how your new truth *feels*.

To connect with this new truth on a feeling level, do some conscious heart-centered breathing (*heart breath*) while affirming your new truth. Practicing conscious breathing in a manner such as the heart breath enhances your emotional state. Conscious breathing quiets the mind, relaxes the body, and improves focus. Here's how:

1. Shift your attention to your heart area.
2. Imagine your breath flowing in and out of your heart area.
3. Breathe more deeply, rhythmically, and slowly.
4. As you are breathing, feel your heart's gratitude that you have reconnected with it by thinking of something or someone you appreciate.
5. Hold that feeling of gratitude while continuing this heart breath for a few more minutes.

Continue to affirm your new truth by acting as if your new belief is true. Identify what you will be doing when you are confident, what you will be doing when you eat healthy, what you will be doing when you live from your heart, and then plan to take that action and engage in that behavior.

Reflect on your responses to this exercise: What came up for you as you were doing it? Did you experience any difficulty creating a strong enough new truth to replace the negative belief with?

Now, write a commitment statement that outlines what you are willing to do to reconnect with your heart using your new truth, conscious breathing, and the actions you will take to strengthen your new truth. Use conscious breathing as you write this commitment statement in your journal.

→ Practice: Old Lies, New Truths Collage Work

For this practice, you will need old magazines, scissors, glue, and heavy stock paper (or a journal if the pages are large enough). Look through the magazines and find sentences, words, and images that reflect the new truths you are creating for yourself. Cut them out of the magazines and glue them to your paper in whatever arrangement you like and filling up as much space as you'd like. When you've completed your collage, share it with the group or, if you've done this activity alone, share it with at least three people who support your Heart Reconnection journey.

Place your new truths collage in a place where you will see it daily. Commit to saying these new truths to yourself at least twice daily while breathing consciously in the manner you learned in the previous exercise.

The only way to change the old lies is to replace them with new truths.

The only way to change the old lies is to replace them with new truths.

→ Practice: Life Story—Past, Present, and Future

Austrian neurologist, psychiatrist, and author Viktor Frankl wrote *Man's Search for Meaning,* chronicling his experiences in an Auschwitz concentration camp during World War II. Frankl is quoted as saying, "When we are no longer able to change a situation, we are challenged to change ourselves." His therapeutic approach, logotherapy, was founded upon the belief that it is the striving to find meaning in one's life that is the primary, most powerful motivating and driving force in humans.

Writing a story about your life often helps you find meaning and value in your experiences. Use your journal for this exercise and take as much time as you need.

- **The past**—Write the story of your past. Include the spoken and unspoken messages you got (directly or indirectly) about yourself from your family, culture, religion, community, and/or teachers as well as events or challenges you've overcome. What personal attributes or strengths enabled you to overcome the challenges you faced?

- **The present**—Continue your story, describing your life and who you are now. Notice and write about how you are different from how you were in the past. Write about how you choose to live your life today and what's important to you. Include challenges you may be experiencing and what you need to help you understand the value of these challenges.

- **The future**—Now finish your story with affirmations about your future self. Start with the question, "What does my heart desire?" Write about your future self using "I am" statements rather than "I will be" statements to begin affirming your heart's desire.

→ Practice: Commitment to Change Letter

Using your work from the previous two practices as your foundation, write a letter to yourself describing in detail the pain you've suffered as a result of old lies and your commitment to change. Really allow yourself an opportunity to reflect on the level of your commitment to changing. Are you willing to go to any lengths to create the life you deserve?

➔ Practice: Personal Mission Statement

A personal mission statement provides some boundaries, enabling us to create and live a life we choose. Everything we do—from relationships to ways we spend our time—can fit within the boundaries of that mission statement. A heart-centered, meaningful personal mission statement isn't always easy to come up with. Base this statement on your answer to "What does my heart desire?" Here are some additional questions to ask yourself to help you write your personal mission statement:

1. **What is important to me?** Identify your core values, qualities that are important to you in your personal and professional life. How is your life connected to those values? (See "List of Values" on pages 153–154 to help you start identifying your core values.)

2. **Where do I want to go?** You can answer this question many different ways—consider your spiritual, mental, or physical desires. This question is purposely open ended to allow you room for creative thinking and discovery.

3. **What does my life look like to me?** Dream big and visualize, in as much detail as possible, what you will be doing when you are living according to your heart's desire.

4. **How do I want to act?** Think of a few words or statements you would want to come to mind when people hear your name or think about you.

5. **What kind of legacy would I like to leave behind?** Imagine that 100 years have passed. In what ways have you impacted the world? What does your impact look like?

Record your answers to these questions in your journal and spend some time reflecting on them. Here are some tips for writing your personal mission statement:

- Keep it simple. Shoot for one or two sentences (focusing on a life that is lived with focus on what matters most).
- Don't forget about others. Yes, this is a *personal* mission statement, but your focus may be just as much about the people you want to impact as it is about yourself.
- Make changes to your mission statement as desired as you continue your Heart Reconnection journey.

Once you have written your personal mission statement, share it with your group and/or counselor as well as with people who are most important to you and support you on your healing path. Get feedback from those you love and/or appreciate who live their lives in ways you respect.

As long as you are staying true to your mission statement, you can't go wrong. Use your personal mission statement to help you make decisions. For example, if you are faced with an opportunity or challenge and it isn't immediately clear to you how you should or want to respond, consider if that opportunity or challenge is aligned with your mission statement. Consider if this opportunity, request, project, challenge, or choice supports these three things: 1) who I am, 2) who I am working to become, and 3) my purpose in life.

LIST OF VALUES

This list of values is a starting point for identifying which qualities are most impor-tant to you to uphold in your life or strive for. There are many, many more values, so feel free to add any other qualities that are important to you. Choose your top five and then place them in order of importance to you in your journal.

ACCOUNTABILITY	AUTHENTICITY	ADVENTURE	AUTONOMY
BALANCE	BEAUTY	BOLDNESS	BRAVERY
CALMNESS	COMPASSION	COMMUNITY	COMPETENCY
CONTRIBUTION	COOPERATION	COURAGE	CREATIVITY
CURIOSITY	DEPENDABILITY	DETERMINATION	DIVERSITY
ENJOYMENT	ENTHUSIASM	EQUALITY	FAIRNESS
FAITH	FAME	FRIENDSHIP	FUN
GENEROSITY	GOODNESS	GRATEFULNESS	GROWTH
HAPPINESS	HARMONY	HEALTH	HONESTY
HUMILITY	HUMOR	INDEPENDENCE	INFLUENCE
JOY	JUSTICE	KINDNESS	KNOWLEDGE
LEADERSHIP	LEARNING	LOVE	LOYALTY
MEANING	MINDFULNESS	OPENNESS	OPTIMISM
ORIGINALITY	PEACE	PLEASURE	POPULARITY
RECOGNITION	RELATIONSHIPS	RELIGION	REPUTATION
RESPECT	RESPONSIBILITY	SECURITY	SELF-RELIANCE
SELF-RESPECT	SERVICE	SPIRITUALITY	STABILITY

STRENGTH	SUCCESS	STATUS	TEAMWORK
TOLERANCE	TRUTH	TRUSTWORTHINESS	UNDERSTANDING
UNITY	VITALITY	WEALTH	WELL-BEING
WISDOM	WORK		

Topic: The Heart-Brain Connection

The Teaching: On a daily basis, the heart and brain are in constant communication, conversing back and forth. Typically operating at the subconscious level, this two-way dialogue of emotion-based signals between the heart and the brain is referred to as the heart-brain connection. We have known about the heart-brain connection for over a century. In 1872, naturalist Charles Darwin, best known for his theory of evolution and the process of natural selection, acknowledged the dynamic neural relationship between the heart and the brain in his book *The Expression of Emotions in Man and Animals.* He wrote,

> [W]hen the heart is affected it reacts on the brain; and the state of the brain again reacts through the pneumogastric [vagus] nerve on the heart; so that under any excitement there will be much mutual action and reaction between these, the two most important organs of the body.

The heart-brain connection is important to understand in the healing process because when we're experiencing stress or what we typically call negative emotions, the heart's input to the brain has a profound effect on the brain's emotional processes by reinforcing the emotional experience and influencing the types of chemicals the brain releases into the rest of the body.

When we feel these "negative" emotions (for example, anger, hate, shame, etc.), the heart sends a signal to the brain mirroring these feelings. These emotions tend to be somewhat irregular and feel chaotic, and so the signal sent to the brain is also somewhat irregular and chaotic. This type of signal is interpreted as stress, which triggers the amygdala, a part of the brain that is located deep in the center of the limbic system, where emotions are controlled. The amygdala is constantly alert to our basic survival needs and readies aversive cues so that our body is ready to fight, flee, or freeze.

To regain the wholeness that is our birthright, we can start to establish a more harmonious heart-brain connection. We can do this by practicing loving-kindness, compassion, gratitude, appreciation, and love. Fear and the need to activate the survival response are lessened as we engage in these practices.

→ Practice: Reclaiming What Has Always Been Yours— Tapping into Your Heart's Wisdom

This practice teaches us how to tap into the heart's wisdom by asking a question of the heart and learning to listen to the innate wisdom inside us. Your question can be anything that's on your mind, but it is best to keep the question short and simple.

This way of tapping into the heart's wisdom is not analytic questioning; it is not about figuring out the "why" or "how" of something. Rather, this practice facilitates an awareness of the thoughts and feelings in the present moment. Here's how:

1. Close your eyes and bring your attention inward.
2. For two to three minutes, practice heart breath (see page 148).

3. As you breathe, bring awareness to your heart, slow your breathing, and invite into your heart area the feeling of loving-kindness, compassion, appreciation, or gratitude. Allow that feeling to fill the heart space completely.

4. As you continue to breathe, ask your heart the question you want to ask.

5. Quietly listen for your heart's wisdom.

Reflecting on your experience, what did you notice in your body after you asked your heart the question? In your journal, jot down any words, pictures, feelings, or body sensations you noticed. Perhaps these things have given you clarity around your question. But be patient. The heart wisdom you seek is within you and will rise to the surface.

→ Practice: Heart-Chakra Connection

In yoga, the heart chakra is one of the seven main centers through which energy flows. It is located in the center of your chest just above your heart. Connecting to your heart chakra cultivates joy, love, and inner peace. Here's how:

1. Sit or lie in a comfortable position.

2. Close your eyes, take a few deep breaths, and let your body relax …letting your shoulders drop down as you continue breathing deeply, rhythmically, from the belly… (pause)

3. Locate any source of negativity or stress you may be experiencing.

4. With a slow deep breath in, consciously breathe that negativity, tension, tightness, or stress into your heart where it can be transformed.

5. Slowly breathe out love and feel a soft peaceful energy settle into that negative source.

6. Continue this practice for 3 to 5 minutes (working up to at least 10 minutes), taking notice of any energy shifts.

7. Now, visualize a sphere of light surrounding your body, protecting your body and heart from any negative source.

8. Breathe again into your heart and visualize a small ball of radiating golden light in your heart.

Practice this meditation daily and set an intention to keep your awareness on the light in your heart chakra throughout the day. Notice the warmth in your body as you do so.

CONSCIOUS BREATHING

From your first breath at birth to your last breath at death, the breath is always with you. You can use the power and skill of conscious breathing to awaken your creative energy and to feel more centered and grounded, more relaxed and focused, or more alive and energized.

There are many different breath practices that, when practiced daily, can enrich your life and enhance your well-being. Conscious breathing is breathing with awareness and incorporating all three breathing spaces into the practice. The three breathing spaces are:

1. The lower breathing space—from the pubic bone to your belly button.

2. The middle breathing space—from the belly button to the nipple line.

3. The upper breathing space—from the nipple line to the collarbones.

Practice breathing into each space. Then practice filling the spaces from the bottom first, the middle, and then the top. (If you practice yoga, you may know this as the full yogic breath.)

Remember that half of your lungs are in the back, not just in the front. So, breathe into your back as well as your chest. Breathe low and slow.

You may have noticed that your breath tends to be quick and shallow, high in the chest when you are tense, anxious, or afraid. The breath becomes ragged and chaotic, reflecting your emotional state. Diaphragmatic, or belly, breathing can help reduce or manage stress because it is calming, balancing, and grounding. Here are three ways to slow your breathing:

Increase the length of the pause after you exhale (meaning postpone your inhale).

Stretch out your breaths so that each inhale and each exhale lasts for 5 to 8 seconds or more. (Gradually build up to this.)

Inhale through your nose and purse your lips so that you exhale as if you were blowing your breath through a straw.

→ Practice: Connecting the Breath to Thought and Affirmations to Change Beliefs

You can change your thoughts and beliefs by creating new, positive, affirming thoughts, breathing them into reality and creating new life experiences. Before starting your breath practice, make a list of new affirming thoughts you would like to believe instead of the negative beliefs that have kept you stuck.

As you begin your breath practice, start by thinking or saying your new thought (new truth) to yourself as you inhale, and as you exhale say to yourself "and so it is." Do this repeatedly in one breath practice session. Commit to doing this practice several times throughout the day and notice any shifts that take place in your thinking over time.

→ Practice: Combining the Breath and Visualization

You can manifest what you want by imagining how you want your life to look, what you'll be doing, and where you'll be doing it. Visualization is a powerful manifestation practice. To combine the breath with visualization, deeply relax your body and mind by consciously breathing while imagining what you desire in as much exacting detail as possible. Here's how:

1. As you inhale, imagine light coming into you and filling your entire body, especially in the heart space.
2. As you exhale, imagine this light radiating from you, flowing into every cell in your body—nourishing, cleansing, renewing, soothing, strengthening.
3. Next, imagine this light emanating out into the world as love, touching and blessing everyone and everything in your life and the universe.
4. Now visualize how you want your life to look, what you'll be doing, and where you'll be doing it in as much detail as possible.

What we give our attention to gets bigger, so do this practice consistently to create the life you want.

→ Practice: Combining the Breath and Movement

Music and movement can enhance your breathing practice and make it even more powerful. Play soft, gentle music, drumming, harp, piano, and so on—whatever you like. As you inhale, feel the expansion of your lungs and move your hands and arms to express this expansion. As you exhale, allow your hands and arms to glide down. Keeping in sync with your breath, move your body in whatever way you wish as the music plays.

You can also practice breathing in rhythm to your footsteps as you walk or run. Notice the felt sense experience as your breath flows with your footsteps.

Another way to combine breath and movement is in a seated position. As you inhale, arch your back and lift your head. As you breathe out, lower your chin and curl your spine. Notice the felt sense experience as your body opens up and collapses with your breath.

→ Practice: Combining the Breath with Sound

Mantras are words (om) or sounds (ahhhh) that are often combined with the breath. Chanting a mantra or toning (sound healing) are also useful in combination with breath practice. You can make all sorts of sounds using your breath. The noises can be calm and soothing like ocean waves or more forceful like the wind to move energy more actively through the body. Take a deep breath into your belly, and for the full length of the out breath, make or chant your sound.

→ Practice: Act of Courage Journal Activity

In your journal, answer the following questions: "What act(s) of courage could I take right now to live more fully from my heart?" and "What stops me from taking this act of courage?"

When you are finished responding to these questions, share your answers with the group or a few people who support your Heart Reconnection journey, and come up with one action you are ready and willing to take to live more fully from your heart.

This practice can also be done experientially with each group member acting out events in a psychodrama related to the barrier to taking the act of courage. Empty chair work can also be useful for expressing the answers to these questions.

→ Practice: Letter from Your Future Self to Your Present Self

Write a letter to yourself from your future self describing the changes that have happened in your life since taking that act of courage you identified in the previous practice. In this letter, describe in as much detail as possible the steps you took along the way and the felt sense experience of the journey as you took each step.

→ Practice: Your Gratitude Jar

A daily gratitude practice can profoundly affect your transformation and the practice of living from your heart. The materials you will need for this practice are a jar or box, decorations (stickers, glitter, ribbon, paint, etc.), colored paper, a pen for writing gratitude notes, and gratitude.

Decorate your jar or box as ornately or as simply as you would like to. Keep it in a place where you will see it every day.

On a daily basis (morning, afternoon, evening, or before bed), think of at least five things you are grateful for. These things can be something as ordinary as the sun shining or as significant as feeling loved. Write down the five things on small strips of paper and place them in your gratitude jar or box. If you are feeling sad, down, or discouraged (or at least once a week), select a few notes from the jar and read them. Notice the felt sense experience going on in your body as you read your notes of gratitude.

→ Practice: Loving-Kindness Meditation

Loving-kindness meditation calms the mind and connects us to the heart. The wonderful thing about this practice is that it can be practiced anywhere. You may notice that as you silently practice this meditation when you're with other people, you begin to feel a connection. Although we use words, images, and feelings in this meditation, the focus of the meditation is on the felt sense of loving-kindness and friendliness toward ourselves and others. We begin with ourselves because we can't offer love to others if we don't love ourselves. Through repetition, we are stating an intention deep within our hearts. Here's how:

1. **Sit quietly and comfortably.** Find a comfortable position and let your body relax. Breathe naturally and notice yourself as you sit and breathe. Let go of any distracting thoughts and focus on your breathing for several minutes.

2. **Bring your attention to your heart space.** Let your heart soften as you bring your attention to your chest and the area around your heart. Breathe gently and silently say to yourself the following:

   May I be filled with loving-kindness.
   May I be safe from inner and outer dangers.
   May I be well in body and mind.
   May I be at ease and happy.

   Repeating these statements, picture yourself as you are now, and hold that image in a heart of loving-kindness. Experience the feelings of warmth and love throughout your body. Repeat these statements over and over again, noticing the felt-sense experience and letting the feelings permeate your body and mind. It may be helpful to spend several weeks focused on cultivating loving-kindness for yourself before expanding your meditation to include others.

3. **Bring into your mind someone you care about and respect.** After focusing on yourself for five to ten minutes, picture in your mind's eye someone you love and care for, who has also loved and cared for you. As you hold the image of this person in your mind, silently say to yourself:

   May you be filled with loving-kindness.
   May you be safe from inner and outer dangers.
   May you be well in body and mind.
   May you be at ease and happy.

   As you do this practice, let whatever arises come up and lovingly continue repeating the statements and notice the felt sense of the experience.

4. **Bring to mind someone you feel neutral about.** Now bring to mind someone you don't know well and feel neutral about. This could be someone you see in a meeting or who works in another department at work. Repeat the same statements, sending feelings of warmth and caring as you say the following:

   May you be filled with loving-kindness.
   May you be safe from inner and outer dangers.
   May you be well in body and mind.
   May you be at ease and happy.

5. **Now bring to mind someone you find irritating or annoying.** Bring into your mind's eye someone you recently got mildly irritated with. Send them feelings of warmth and caring as you silently say these statements:

> *May you be filled with loving-kindness.*
> *May you be safe from inner and outer dangers.*
> *May you be well in body and mind.*
> *May you be at ease and happy.*

6. **Extend your meditation to include others as well as animals and the planet.** Send all creatures feelings of warmth and caring as you silently say these statements:

> *May you be filled with loving-kindness.*
> *May you be safe from inner and outer dangers.*
> *May you be well in body and mind.*
> *May you be at ease and happy.*

Take time to notice your heart throughout the practice. Loving-kindness meditation will take practice. As your heart begins to open, you will notice that you enjoy living wholeheartedly and will want to keep your heart open instead of closed and protected.

➜ Practice: Write a Letter to Yourself from Your Pain

Using your journal, take some time to identify the emotional pain that keeps you stuck and closed down. Ask yourself, "What makes my heart hurt?" Is it a pattern of behavior, a belief, a thought, or a situation? Did someone say something to you that was hurtful? Once you've had time to reflect on this, the next step is to write a letter to your pain.

Before inviting your "pain" to write you a letter, take a few deep breaths to ground and center yourself. When you are ready, step in to an *observer perspective* and watch while you picture yourself in your emotional pain. Give yourself time and space to observe any felt-sense experiences in your body and how your mind responds to the felt sense of the emotional pain.

Remember that what you're experiencing are simply sensations and thoughts about the pain you've experienced. From the observer perspective, you have the ability to choose what action to take to eliminate the emotional pain, and the more you practice this observer perspective, the more you develop the ability to redefine the pain you are feeling.

Once you've done this, invite your pain to write you a letter. If you find it difficult to find a voice for your pain, you can begin by picturing what the pain looks like: What color is it? What kind of shape does it have? Where is it located in your body? If it could make a sound, what would that sound like? Is there something the pain is trying to tell you?

Use your journal as you reflect on these questions and begin your letter from the pain's voice.

Your pain is a divine rite of passage
through which you will be reborn as a being
of strength, wisdom and purpose.

~Bryant McGill

→ Practice: Letting Go of Pain Ceremony

A medicine wheel altar is created in the shape of a circle with four distinct parts (see the medicine wheel on page 38 in chapter 5). There are many ways to make a medicine wheel altar, but for the purposes of this exercise, a simple altar is fine. You can use a medicine wheel altar as the foundation for any number of practices, including meditation, reflection, and contemplation, and in conjunction with the teachings in the main body of this book for each of the directions. In this practice, it will serve as a place for participants to place the ancestral messages that have been weighing them down in the position of the north (which represents a time of honor for the elders).

To create the medicine wheel altar for this ceremony, place four stones around the circumference of a circle, representing each of the four directions: east, south, west, and north. Place a stone in the center if you wish, symbolizing the creator and the meeting point between the visible and invisible realms, and smaller stones between the four stones to outline the circle.

In a tear-out page of your journal, you will write down painful messages received or absorbed from family (spoken and unspoken) that you have been carrying around. These messages can be shared aloud with the group before being placed on the altar.

Playing music that signifies release, and letting go can enhance this activity. "Amazing Grace" is a good choice. There's a powerful version by the group Celtic Woman you might want to check out. You can also use movement and dance to let go of these old painful messages that have been weighing you down.

Repeat this process to replace the old, painful messages with new, joyful messages. Play music that signifies moving forward, using movement/dance to celebrate the new messages that you are creating for future generations.

Topic: Finding Your Balance and Spiritual Center

The Teaching: The true basis of love is acceptance. When we are centered spiritually, we simply accept what is. There are no conditions. Our spiritual center is a sacred place within ourselves where we find mental, physical and emotional peace, a place where we feel at ease with ourselves and our environment. Part of finding your center involves becoming aware of the spiritual nature that guides you. There are many ways to do this, a few of which are included here.

→ Practice: Assessing Your Life Balance

This practice brings awareness to your current life balance so that you can make a conscious decision to rebalance areas that may be off-kilter and find your center. Photocopy the "Wheel of Life" image on page 168 or recreate it on a blank piece of paper.

1. **Brainstorm your life areas.** Close your eyes and take a few deep breaths. Then consider about eight areas of your life that are most important to you. This could be the things you value most in your life such as family, friends, leisure/fun, financial, career, physical health, emotional health, spiritual, etc. Write these down on the wheel, one on each "spoke."

2. **Assess each area.** Rate the level of attention you are currently devoting to each area, using a scale of 0 (low) to 10 (high). Mark each score on the appropriate spoke of your wheel.

3. **Connect the marks.** Connect the marks around the circle. Does your life wheel look and feel balanced to you? Are you spending time in the areas you want to spend time in?

4. **Think about what your heart desires.** As you pause and reflect on what your heart desires and how you want to live your life, consider what your ideal level in each area of your life might be if you were living connected to your heart. Remember that balance doesn't necessarily mean "5" in each life area. Plot your ideal scores around your wheel as well.

5. **Take action.** Looking at the visual map of your current life balance compared to your ideal life balance, where do you want to focus your attention? Remember that what we place our attention on gets bigger. Once you've decided where you want to focus your attention, identify actions that you are ready to take to begin regaining balance. Commit to these actions in writing and find a like-minded partner or group to be accountable to.

→ Practice: Contemplative Prayer

Contemplative prayer is a spiritual discipline that is similar to mantra meditation; although it has roots in Christianity, you don't need to be Christian to practice it. Here you choose your own sacred word such as *Calm, Buddha, Faith, Father, Hallelujah, Jesus, Lord, Love, Mary, Mercy, Mother, Om, Peace, Silence, Stillness, Trust, Yes* —whatever you choose. You will use this sacred word throughout the practice. If you don't want to use a sacred word, focus on your heart space instead.

1. Find a quiet place free from distraction or interruption. Plan to spend at least 10 minutes on the practice, building up to 30 minutes as you continue the practice.
2. Sit in a comfortable position and take several breaths.
3. If using a sacred word, bring it to mind.

4. When you are comfortable, close your eyes.

5. Begin by silently repeating your sacred word or focusing on your heart space.

6. When thoughts come into your mind, gently bring your attention back to your sacred word (or heart space) and visualize all thoughts floating by.

7. When the time has passed, keep your eyes closed for a few minutes and sit in stillness before getting up.

As with many of the practices included in this book, contemplative prayer can bring up feelings and wounds that may be buried deep within the psyche. If you are establishing a contemplative prayer practice alone (or any of these practices), please make sure you have support in case memories surface during the practice. Teachers and guides: please make sure participants in your groups and sessions are aware of this.

→ Practice: Mandala Meditation to Open Your Heart

A mandala is a spiritual symbol, usually geometric, in Hinduism and Buddhism, but you don't have to be of either of those traditions to create a mandala of your own. For this practice, you will need paper and colored pencils, markers, or pastels. Before you begin creating your mandala, start with this brief meditation:

1. Sit or lie down in a comfortable position.

2. Gently close your eyes and take a few deep breaths... (pause)

3. With each exhalation, feel your body relax more and more ... (pause)

4. Now take a few more deep breaths and feel your mind relax along with your body... slowing down your thoughts and

just noticing these thoughts floating by easily and effort-lessly... (pause) allowing your mind to let go of any particular focus and turning inward to that deep place within you that desires healing... (pause)

5. Breathing in... Breathing out... (pause)

6. Breathing in... Breathing out... (pause)

7. Now, place one hand on your heart and one hand on your belly... (pause)

8. And as you continue to breathe in and out, notice the warmth of your hands on your heart and your belly... (pause)

9. Notice how this warmth feels... (pause)

10. Imagine the warmth from your hands helping to open your heart and belly... allowing oxygen and nutrients that help healing to flow freely through the blood vessels... (pause)

11. Now return your awareness to the here and now... when you are ready, gently open your eyes and reorient yourself to the room.

Using colored pencils, markers, or pastels, draw your heart mandala. The heart may be at the center of the mandala or incorporated throughout the heart mandala design; it's up to you to listen to your heart and let what you hear come through.

Journal your experience from the felt-sense experience rather than from your head and share your experiences with the group or those who support you on your Heart Reconnection journey.

→ **Practice: Spiritual Center Meditation**

Before beginning this meditation, think about your own personal spirituality. Think about what gives you meaning and purpose. Now, select a word or a short phrase (five words or less) that is meaningful to you and can be repeated within the time it takes to exhale. Silently repeat this word or phrase during the meditation.

Teacher, recite the following to lead others or record the script and play back. Do not say the numerals aloud; they are only included as a guide. Be sure to allow enough time for each step to be implemented before going on to the next step. Ellipses represent pauses.

1. *Close your eyes or focus your gaze gently at a 45-degree angle. Start by relaxing your muscles. When thoughts come to mind, let them go, and turn your attention back to your body.*

2. *Let your muscles become loose and relaxed, starting with your feet... your ankles... lower legs... knees... upper legs... pelvis... torso ...back... shoulders... arms... hands... face... and head.*

3. *Feel your body... loose and relaxed....*

4. *Turn your attention now to your breathing. Notice each breath, without trying to change your breathing in any way...Just observe....As thoughts arise, acknowledge them and let them go, returning your attention to your breathing ...*

5. *Breathe naturally... slowly ...*

6. *As your thoughts wander, simply return your attention to your breathing.*

7. *Notice your breath as it flows gently in and out of your body... without any effort ...*

8. Acknowledge your thoughts and focus again on your breathing . . . interruptions will happen . . . just let these thoughts go and return your attention to your breathing . . .

9. Now think of the meaningful word or phrase you selected . . . and say this word or phrase in your mind as you exhale . . .

10. Each time you breathe out, say the word or the phrase . . .

11. As your thoughts wander, bring your attention again to repeating your meaningful statement with each out breath.

12. Continue repeating the word or phrase each time you exhale . . .

13. Bring your attention back to the word or phrase you are repeating with each gentle breath out . . .

14. With gentle acceptance, continue to focus on the word or phrase, repeating it each time you breathe out . . . allowing distracting thoughts to float by . . .

15. Now slowly begin to bring your awareness to the present moment . . . and turn your attention to your breathing. Notice your calm, smooth breaths . . . in and out. . . . Allow your awareness to turn now to your body . . . calm and relaxed. . . . Notice how your body feels . . . become more aware of your surroundings . . .

16. Let your attention turn now to your thoughts . . . back to normal conscious awareness . . . normal attention to thoughts . . .

17. Sit quietly for a moment with your eyes open . . . enjoying the feeling of relaxation while bringing your attention . . . your awareness back to the present moment . . .

18. Reflect upon the experience of meditation . . . notice what it was like . . . notice how you feel now . . . without judgment . . . knowing that whatever happened was meaningful and natural.

→ Practice: Write Your Own Eulogy

Death is separation. A physical death is the separation of the soul from the body, and spiritual death is the separation of the soul from the divine (however you define it—e.g., God, Spirit, Universe, Higher Power, etc.). A eulogy is a funeral oration or memorial speech given in memory of someone who has recently died as a way of paying tribute to the deceased.

This exercise is about recognizing the spiritual death many of us experience in which our soul has become separated from our heart center and source of love. Remember back to when you began feeling separate from the divine and what that separation felt like. A brief meditation can help achieve a reflective frame of mind.

In your journal, write a eulogy about the spiritual death you have experienced. When you are finished, share your eulogy with the rest of the group or people who support you on your Heart Reconnection journey. What was it like to think and write about your life and spiritual death?

→ Practice: The Nine Contemplations of Atisha (Practice by Joan Halifax Roshi)

Atisha was an eleventh-century Tibetan Buddhist scholar who systematized the method for generating an enlightened mind. These nine contemplations (see pages 175–176) come from Atisha and offer a way to explore the inevitability of death and what is important to us in the light of our mortality. The practice asks us to question what we are doing in our life at this very moment and to see what is important for us to do in order to prepare for death. Read the Nine Contemplations.

Pair up with a partner and find a comfortable place to sit, making sure your body is relaxed and calm. The following is the leader's script:

These nine contemplations remind us about the nature of life and death. Decide who is going to read first.

Make eye contact with your partner as you are ready (if you are being read to, you can close your eyes if you want to as your partner reads to you). Let your mind settle. Bring your attention to your breath.

Readers, slowly read each of the nine contemplations to your partner over and over until time is called, starting with Dear Friend…For example, "Dear Friend…all of us will die sooner or later…" and "Dear Friend…your life span is decreasing continuously…" Receiver: as your partner reads the nine contemplations to you, please consider them deeply.

After 4 to 5 minutes (or however long you desire), the listener and receiver switch roles. Process the experience.[4]

THE NINE CONTEMPLATIONS OF ATISHA

(Dear friend…) All of Us Will Die Sooner or Later

(Dear friend…) Your Life Span Is Decreasing Continuously

(Dear friend…) Death Will Come Whether You Are Prepared or Not

---

4 This practice is based on the work of Larry Rosenberg.

(Dear friend…) Your Life Span, Like That of All Living Beings, Is Not Fixed

(Dear friend…) Death Has Many Causes

(Dear friend…) Your Body Is Fragile and Vulnerable

(Dear friend…) Your Loved Ones Cannot Keep You from Death

(Dear friend…) At the Moment of Your Death, Your Material Resources Are of No Use to You

(Dear friend…) Your Own Body Cannot Help You at the Time of Your Death

→ Practice: Write Your Own Birth Announcement

This practice is similar to writing your own eulogy, but instead you are writing about the rebirth, transformation, and reconnection to the heart that is happening as you journey on this path. Take some time to reflect on your journey so far. Write a birth announcement announcing the ways in which you have transformed and rebirthed yourself.

Topic: Present Moment

The Teaching: Who would you be without your past, without your story? Some might say there can't be a present without a past, that who we are today is an accumulation of our past experiences. More accurately, the past as we understand it is not about what actually happened but our thoughts and beliefs about what happened. So, one might say that without a present, there is no past.

Nelson Mandela said, "As I walked out the door toward the gate that would lead to my freedom, I knew if I didn't leave my bitterness and hatred behind, I'd still be in prison." Viktor Frankl, author of *Man's Search for Meaning,* believed that people can survive any hardship if they are able to make a positive meaning out of it. "Even the worst circumstance can be transformed by our minds," he wrote.

Most of the time we are living from memories in our subconscious (conditioned) mind. When we keep our attention on the past, we forfeit our present. The old date in our minds and the emotional charge attached to the past create our continued experience of the same repeating problems. When our mind is emptied of its old contents, we can access wisdom and creative inspiration. Mindshifting enables us to do this.

→ Practice: Mindshift

Reflect on a challenging situation or event that has happened, something you remember as bad, painful, wrong, or negative in some way. Record this experience in your journal.

1. State out loud, "This means nothing except the story I make up about it."
2. Visualize or picture yourself shifting the memory or thought from negative to positive and associate a pleasant feeling or emotion with the new picture. You can do this by recalling a time when you were calm and relaxed.
3. Using all of your senses, visualize as vividly as you can, this experience when you were calm and relaxed.
4. Clear your mind and release all judgments or stories you have made up about the situation.
5. Invite in and be open to higher inspiration, a new perception, and a more positive interpretation.

➜ Practice: Anchoring Mindshift

Anchoring is a neurolinguistic programming (NLP) technique that helps to associate a particular, positive emotional response with a particular phrase or sensation. When you choose a positive emotion or thought and intentionally connect or associate it to a simple gesture, you can activate the anchor any time you want to change how you feel, and your feelings will immediately begin to change.

1. Identify what you want to feel (e.g., confidence, happiness, calmness, etc.).

2. Create that *felt sense* state by recalling a time you felt this positive emotion very strongly.

3. Amplify the image you've recalled, making it sharper, more vivid, and more intense.

4. Select an anchoring phrase or touch (e.g., "I am _____ _____" or touching your first finger and thumb together).

5. Repeat this practice at least once daily, until you find that simply touching your first finger and thumb together or saying your phrase immediately elicits feelings of happiness, confidence, or calm (or whatever positive emotion you identified).

Begin to notice the constant stream of thoughts, or perhaps the negative inner talk that goes on in your head. As you acknowledge your thoughts, remind yourself that they are just that: thoughts. "Observing" your thoughts in this way allows for more space between you and your thoughts, providing an opportunity to change the thought to a positive one.

➔ Practice: Mindful Walking

If you find sitting meditation challenging or you want to try something a little different, try walking meditation. This is an active practice that requires you to be consciously aware and moving in the environment.

Mindful walking is an intentional practice. Begin by becoming aware of your body and how it feels. Bend your knees slightly and feel your hips as your center of gravity. Take a few deep breaths and bring your awareness into the present moment.

1. Now walk slightly slower than your regular pace, maintaining the very slight bend in the knees. As you walk, notice the gentle heel-to-toe rhythm of your feet as each one makes contact with the ground.

2. Breathe naturally and fully. Allow your eyes to focus softly ahead of you, gently observing your surroundings. Maintain this rhythm and breath as you walk.

3. When your attention drifts away from the sensations of walking and breathing, simply notice your thoughts, moods, or feelings without judgment and gently bring your awareness back to the present moment, back to the walking. Do this practice for about 20 minutes.

4. When you're ready to end your walking meditation, come to a gentle standstill. Breathe deeply as you experience yourself standing still, noticing your feet on the ground.

➔ Practice: Mindful Eating

Many of us don't take the time to sit and enjoy our meals. We are frequently rushed and eat on the run. To practice mindful eating, slow down and pay attention to what you're eating. Let your body catch up to your brain. Slowing down is one of the best ways to get our mind and body to communicate what we really need for nutrition. The body doesn't send a satiation signal until about 20 minutes after the brain, which is why we unconsciously overeat.

We also want to pay attention to our eating environment and proactively plan our meals. This provides an opportunity to develop healthy environmental cues about what and how much to eat. Eating at consistent times and places helps your mood and sleep schedule. Plating rather than eating out of containers is also helpful as is sitting at a table instead of multitasking while you are eating.

Know your body's personal hunger signals by becoming aware of your body. Often, we eat when our mind or the clock tells us it's time instead of listening to our hunger cues. Mindful eating involves listening attentively to our body's hunger signals rather than to our mind's signals.

→ Practice: Mindful Conversation

Active listening goes a long way in conversation. Instead of thinking of how you're going to respond in the conversation, focus on listening to what the other person is saying. Listen mindfully to the other person and notice your own inner dialogue. You can practice this in group or with a partner on your journey by taking turns talking and listening.

References

Achterberg, J. (1985). *Imagery in Healing Shamanism and Modern Medicine*. Boston and London: Shambala.

Borysenko, J. (2008). *Your Soul's Compass: What is Spiritual Guidance?* New York: Hay House Inc.

Cordova, V.F. (2007). *How It Is The Native American Philosophy of V.F. Cordova*. Tucson: The University of Arizona Press.

Darwin, Charles. (2017, Reprint Edition) *The Expression of the Emotions in Man and Animals*. Paperback, Reprint Edition. Dover Publications.

Dveirin, G. "The Culture Is the Competence: Evolving the Practice of Treatment and Recovery." *Counselor Magazine*.

Faulkner, M. (2004). *Easy Does It Dating Guide*. Center City, Minnesota. Hazelden.

Faulkner, M. (2007). *Easy Does It Relationship Guide*. Center City, Minnesota. Hazelden.

Lipton, Bruce. "Bruce H. Lipton, Ph.D. in Paris: The Impact of Our Environment and Our State of Mind on Our Health" Bruce Lipton website. *https://www.brucelipton.com/resource/video-and-podcasts/bruce-h-lipton-phd-paris-the-impact-our-environment-and-our-state-mind.*

Monaghan, P. (2000). *The Goddess Companion Daily Meditations on the Feminine Spirit*. St. Paul, MN: Llewellyn.

PBS. *The Good Vibrations of the Quantum Field Theories, The Nature of Reality, the physics of nothing, everything and all things in between. pbs.org*, August 5, 2013.

Pearson, C. (1991). *Awakening the Heroes Within: Twelve Archetypes to Help Us Find Ourselves and Transform Our World*. New York: Harper Collins Publisher.

Peat, F. (2002) *Blackfoot Physics*. Boston: Weisler Books.

Taegel, W. (2012). *The Mother Tongue Intimacy in the Eco-field*. Wimberley, TX: 2nd Tier Publishing.

Thich Nhat Hanh. (1999). *The Heart of the Buddha's Teaching: Transforming Suffering into Peace, Joy, and Liberation*. New York: Penguin Random House, LLC.

Woititz, Janet Geringer. (1983) "13 Characteristics." *Adult Children of Alcoholics*. Pompano Beach, FL: Health Communications.

Spirit Recovery Medicine Bag
Lee McCormick and Mary Faulkner

The Spirit Recovery Meditation Journal
Lee McCormick
Foreword by Don Miguel Ruiz

The Spirit Recovery Medicine Bag and *The Spirit Recovery Meditation Journal* offer readers engaging and informative ways to find more meaning and satisfaction in their lives.

Self-Help / Recovery
Spirit Recovery Medicine Bag
ISBN-13: 9780757317941
eISBN: 9780757317958
$14.95 us

The Spirit Recovery
Meditation Journal
ISBN-13: 9780757321252
ISNB-10: 0757321259
$14.95 us

About the Authors

Mary Faulkner, MA, is a writer, therapist, and teacher. She is the author of eight books on spirituality and healing. Mary is the cofounder of Integrative Life Center; former director of women's services at Cumberland Heights, both in Nashville, Tennessee; former trauma specialist; and a spiritual advisor at The Ranch in Nunnelly, Tennessee. Mary certifies counselors and health care professionals in Integrative Hypnotherapy for Transforming Trauma and Healing the Heart.

Lee McCormick is the founder of The Ranch Recovery Center in Tennessee and The Canyon Treatment Center in Malibu, California. He is also cofounder of Nashville's Integrative Life Center and IOP/PHP Community Recovery program. Through Spirit Recovery Inc., Lee facilitates the production of healing and recovery conferences and spiritual journeys around the world. He is the executive producer of the documentary *Dreaming Heaven*, in which he plays a leading role. He is the author of *The Spirit Recovery Meditation Journal: Meditations for Reclaiming Your Authenticity* and coauthor of *Dreaming Heaven: The Beginning Is Near!* and *Spirit Recovery Medicine Bag*.

Joan Borysenko, PhD, is a pioneer in the integration of mind, body, and spirit. She is a licensed psychologist with a doctorate in cell biology from Harvard ical School, and president of Mind-Body Health Sciences. A *New York Times* ing author of sixteen books and several meditation CDs, Joan synthe- -edge science with deep humanity. She is a world-renowned expert dy connection. Her work has been foundational in an interna- evolution that recognizes the role of meaning and the spiritual an integral part of health and healing.

s in two dimensions. One reflects his lifelong con- Mind/Heart and the other his psychological and scientific research. While both his doctorates concentrate on the synergy of ecopsychology and the matrix of field physics, he counts his shamanic training described in his book *Walking With Bears* as the most important of his life. *Walking With Bears* completes a trilogy that includes *Wild Heart* and *Mother Tongue*; all address a human return to Earth-based consciousness. Will is dean at Wisdom School of Graduate Studies, Ubiquity University, Austin, Texas. He is an experienced psychotherapist with a demonstrated history of working in the education management industry, and holds a doctor of ministry focused in Family Systems Therapy and Spirituality from University of California at Berkeley.

Holly Cook, LPC-MHSP, is a licensed professional counselor and mental health service provider with more than 30 years of experience as a therapist, program administrator, and international trainer. Holly has been described as a "life artist" who works with people, helping them find and create the life they want to live. In addition to her private practice in Nashville, Tennessee, Holly is a cofounder of the Integrative Life Center, which integrates spirit and science-based approaches to healing and creating community.

Gary Seidler is the consulting executive editor to *Counselor* magazine, a peer-reviewed journal for professionals in the mental health and addiction fields. He is the cofounder of Health Communications, Inc., a leading self-help, wellness, and recovery publisher, and the cofounder/codirector of US Journal Training, a quality provider of continuing education courses and conferences for mental health professionals.